Get Off To A Winning Start In Network Marketing

David Barber

Insight Network Marketing Library

Get Off To A Winning Start in Network Marketing
David Barber

Insight Publishing Ltd
Sterling House
Church Street
Ross-on-Wye
Herefordshire
HR9 5HN

Phone: 01989-564496
Fax: 01989-565596

Notice of Liability
While great care has been taken in the preparation of this
publication, it should not be used as a substitute for appropriate
professional advice. Neither the author nor Insight Publishing can
accept any liability for loss or damage occasioned by any person
acting as a result of the material in this book.

ISBN: 1-899298-03-7

Cover design by Just Proportion, Louth, Lincolnshire
Cartoons by James Hutcheson Design, Edinburgh
Printed in Finland by WSOY

Contents

Get Off To A Flying Start!

'The greater the action the greater the success. The sooner you act, the quicker you will get there.'

So let's get some action going *now*! First, get as much support as you can! *If you have someone experienced working closely with you, follow their advice.* If your sponsor is unable to support you, keep going upline till you find someone who can.

But, if you can't arrange for any practical help, don't worry! Many people have become winners without upline support—it's just harder, that's all. Try to link up with a co-learner—a distributor who, like yourself, is just starting out. It will help you both to work through that critical period until you get your first distributor on board.

Above all, get active! The best way to *learn* is to *do* and network marketing works best for those who just get on with it. This action list will get you off on the right lines:

1   Complete the formalities with your sponsor

2   Learn the Distributor Pack thoroughly

3   Invest in a good range of samples and practise until you can show them well

4   Order any sponsoring aids (leaflets, tapes & videos) recommended by your sponsor

5   Write out your Goals Sheet, as I advise in Chapter 3

6   Decide how much time you will give to the business

7   Decide your short- and long-term income targets and get advice on how realistic they are, given the time you are committing

8   Set a retailing target (see page 159)

9   Write out your Contact List as I advise in Chapter 8

10 Start making those first contacts immediately (following the advice in Chapter 11) either with the support of your upline or, if you are on your own, once you have read this book twice

11 Set a target for how many people you will phone each day to arrange a meeting and keep to it

12 Tackle your first Two-to-One sponsoring meetings as explained in Chapter 12

13 Go to the next training for new distributors and attend as many other trainings and meetings as possible. Home in on successful distributors and pick their brains

14 If your company has opportunity meetings or business briefings, support yours every week

15 Order your first books, tapes and videos on network marketing, your opportunity and personal development

16 Make it a habit to spend at least thirty minutes a day, every day, studying your learning materials

17 Start reading and applying a good book on personal development as soon as possible

18 As soon as you have sponsored your first person:
(a) Take them through this checklist
(b) Take them through this book
(c) Work closely with them as I advise in Chapter 15

19 When you have two or three people signed up, start a regular weekly meeting with them, pooling your knowledge and helping each other out.

As I said at the start of this action list:

The greater the action the greater the success. The sooner you act, the quicker you will get there!

Introduction

Welcome To The S.T.A.R. Leadership Programme

Welcome to our wonderful industry of network marketing! You now have a real opportunity to create a life that most can only dream of: the freedom to be your own boss, the chance to make your dearest hopes come true, the opportunity to do the same for many others, the potential to create financial security and the time to enjoy it!

Through the S.T.A.R. Leadership Programme I will show you the way to achieve this and more. I will show you how to truly open up the way to your success.

The real secret of success in this business

Have you heard the saying: *Anyone and everyone can succeed in network marketing. This is truly a business for everyone*? Let me make it clear what this means. Network marketing has never made anyone successful; it is distributors, people just like yourself, who grasp the opportunity and make *themselves* successful *by properly applying the network marketing concept*. So who can succeed in network marketing?

- People who cannot read or write have built successful businesses
- People with almost no education have built successful businesses
- People who have been out of the job market for twenty years bringing up their children have built successful businesses
- People with no previous business, commercial or management experience have built successful businesses
- People from deprived backgrounds have built successful businesses

- People who are the 'wrong' race, colour, sex or age have built successful businesses
- People with no money and crippling debts have built successful businesses
- People who on their own admission are not very clever and are slow at learning have built successful businesses
- People with all of those problems combined have built successful businesses.

If they could succeed, do you think you can? Yet, it is undeniable, very many people have failed:

- Yes, certainly, people from all the above backgrounds have failed
- So have high-level businesspeople and professionals
- So have wealthy people or people from privileged backgrounds
- So have well-connected people
- So have previously highly successful entrepreneurs
- So have top-flight salespeople.

What was the difference? Just this: those in the first group *learnt and applied the business properly*; those in the second did not. This may sound too simple to be true, but you will discover for yourself that:

> **In this business, it is not what you've got that matters, it is what you *learn*, what you *do* and *how* you do it**

How to Get On-Track for success

In any field of human endeavour you must focus on the three elements of all success: **Action**, **Attitude** and **Knowledge**.

ACTION is the objective because, without action, nothing happens—there can be no success. But what *makes* you act, *how much* action you take, *how determined* you are to keep acting and *how successful* your actions are, all depend on your ATTITUDES. In terms of aiming for success, KNOW-LEDGE has only one function and that is to make your actions more effective. Attitudes and knowledge are meaningless unless they are translated into action.

Action is the vehicle, Knowledge is the road-map, your Attitudes are the fuel that will drive you to success

---

There are two popular misconceptions. The first is that having a Positive Mental Attitude (PMA) will make you successful. Unless it is put into action, it will not. Network marketing is full of people with PMA but no action and it is a major cause of failure. The second misconception is the saying: *Knowledge is power*. It is not. Knowledge without action has no power.

This means that you will *only* succeed if you are prepared:

• To learn,
• To apply what you've learnt, *and*
• To apply it with the right attitudes.

As this is the formula for success, I call this **Staying On-Track**. The formula for failure is the opposite and I call it **Going Off-Track**:

• *Not* being prepared to learn, *or*
• *Not* applying what you've learnt, *or*
• *Not* doing it with the right attitudes.

I can show you what to do and how to do it, but to make it all happen what *you* must contribute is your commitment to Stay On-Track. *No one else can do this for you.* If you do not want to Stay On-Track, no trainer anywhere, no upline in your business, can help you. It is said that God helps those who help themselves. So not even God can help those who will not Stay On-Track!

What do you have to learn?

Network marketing is breathtakingly simple. The whole business is based on three very straightforward activities, none of which requires any special talents or previous experience:

1. *Show a simple business opportunity you are proud of* to friends, relations, neighbours or acquaintances, or people introduced to you by them

2. *Show a product you are proud of* to people you know— friends, relations, neighbours or acquaintances, or people introduced to you by them

3. In your own time, and as your confidence, knowledge and experience grow, *in a very simple way, teach people coming into your business to do the same.*

In the language of network marketing, these three activities are known as **Sponsoring**, **Retailing** and **Teaching**.

As we saw above, how *effectively* you carry out these actions is determined by your attitudes to them, so the level of your success will be determined by a fourth activity:

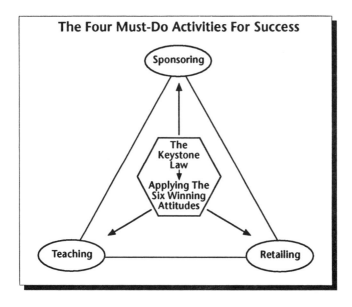

The Four Must-Do Activities For Success
- Sponsoring
- The Keystone Law
- Applying The Six Winning Attitudes
- Teaching
- Retailing

Applying Winning Attitudes. And where sponsoring, retailing and teaching are concerned, we are talking about applying *six* Winning Attitudes.

These four activities (Retailing, Sponsoring, Teaching and Applying The Six Winning Attitudes) are known as **The Four Must-Do Activities For Success**. Focus only on these because they are the only activities which contribute directly to your income. The diagram above shows you the relationship between them.

Sponsoring, Retailing and Teaching form the outer triangle because they are outward activities which involve other people. Applying The Six Winning Attitudes is placed in the centre for two reasons: because this is an inner activity, a question of inner development; and because this is the driving force behind the other three. If you do not apply the right attitudes, it does not matter how much sponsoring, retailing or teaching you do, you are not going to build a strong business.

The Six Winning Attitudes are themselves driven by the **Keystone Law**, the fundamental truth behind network marketing, the understanding of which will be the key to your success. I will explain this to you in Chapter 15, but in the meantime, can you work out what it is for yourself?

So, to summarise, you must learn in a very simple way:

- The basics of how the *concept* works
- How to apply the *Six Winning Attitudes* to your day-to-day activities
- How to *sponsor*
- How to *retail*
- How to *teach* others to do the same

What talents do you need to sponsor, retail and teach?

Sponsoring and retailing are a branch of the sales profession, but not in the traditional sense. There's a lot of twaddle spoken about selling, giving it a mystique and a difficulty which is really not there.

The whole nub of selling is that if you trust someone *enough*, like them *enough* and respect them *enough*, you are much more likely to buy off them. Therefore, the more you can make people trust, like and respect you, the more they are going to buy from you, whether that be your product or your opportunity. These are all qualities which make a wonderful human being and which anyone can develop.

You will see that there is nothing here about having to master complicated sales techniques, nor about being articulate, physically attractive, intelligent or well-educated. Although all these will help if you are trusted, liked and respected, *none of them will make up for a lack of those qualities*.

If people worry about selling it is often because they are not confident they can be persuasive. Persuasion can make a person buy against their better judgement but that is not the true art of selling. Someone who is trusted, liked and respected but lacks the art of persuasion will always sell more than someone who has the art of persuasion but is not trusted, liked or respected. This is just another reason why anyone can succeed in network marketing.

The S.T.A.R. Leadership Programme will show you how to be seen as trustworthy, likeable and demanding of respect. I do cover sales techniques in the programme, but every single one is a technique which anyone can easily learn and apply. This is important to you, particularly if you don't feel confident about selling, but it is even more important to know that you can show *anyone* in your business how to use these techniques, no matter how little selling ability they think they might have.

Again, there is nothing difficult about teaching. The whole nub of *teaching* is that, if you trust someone *enough*, like them *enough* and respect them *enough*, you will learn from them. Therefore, the more you can make people trust, like and respect you, the more willing they will be to learn from you. These are all qualities which make a wonderful human being and which anyone can develop.

You will see that there is nothing here about having to be good at teaching, nor about being articulate, physically attractive, intelligent or well-educated. Although all these will help if you are trusted, liked and respected, *none of them will make up for a lack of those qualities.*

So as you can see, the qualities you need to sponsor and retail well are the very same as the qualities you need to teach well!

How The S.T.A.R. Leadership Programme can help

This book is the first of three in the **S.T.A.R. Leadership Programme**, a fresh approach to home-learning in network marketing. 'S.T.A.R.' stands for Sponsor, Teach, Attitudes, Retail—the Four Must-Do Activities I referred to above. From the first telephone call, the programme will take you step by step through everything you need to know to build a strong, successful business of which you can be truly proud.

I have made the programme simple without being simplistic. There is nothing difficult to learn, but equally, network marketing is not something you can master in a week. If you are truly committed to becoming all you can be in this great industry, you must expect to invest at least six months in learning your new profession. Compared to other high-paying professions, this is little enough to ask.

But there is no need to put any pressure on yourself. Just learn steadily at your own pace and you are sure to get there in the end. So don't open the other books in the programme just yet. This one is specially designed to get you started. Only then should you seek to improve your skills by working through the rest of the programme. If you follow my advice you will, I promise you, master all the techniques much more quickly and easily than you believed possible! But, if you try to rush ahead too quickly, you will only court disaster, just like a novice skier going straight for the advanced runs.

An outline of the book

In Part I of this book, I will introduce you to four of the Six Winning Attitudes: the four personal driving forces which help you to become the person you need to be to succeed.

Then, in Part II, you will learn the practical skills you need to put these attitudes to work and make a winning start at sponsoring and retailing.

Finally, in Part III, you will learn about the vital attitudes which will help you to pass on what you have learnt to other people—the very heart of network marketing.

The best way to learn is to teach

If network marketing is to be truly a business for everyone, you will need to introduce a simple, standardised teaching programme, teaching the winning elements of network marketing in a way which any motivated person can learn. This sounds difficult, but the job is done for you if you introduce the S.T.A.R. Leadership Programme to everyone in your group.

I call it a 'Leadership' Programme because, the minute anyone recruits or 'sponsors' their first person, they become a group leader.

But you can only explain this material to others if you are clear about it for yourself. The Leadership Quiz at the end of each chapter is designed to make this easier for you. If you are like me you will normally skip this kind of thing, but I promise you that you will learn much more quickly if you work at these exercises.

It will also pay you to make short presentations of the key points in each chapter to an experienced upline or a co-learner, a friend, a spouse—or even to yourself if there is no one else around. This too will greatly speed up your learning.

I prepared the S.T.A.R. Leadership Programme with just one thought in mind: to help you and your people to achieve whatever it is you want from this great business. To help you share this material with others, please feel free to use quotations, concepts, diagrams and cartoons from the book in your meetings and trainings. And please, please, send me any ideas you have for making the programme even more useful to you in the vital task of teaching your group!

Finally, I've been there myself, so I know just how you are feeling right now! I know how important this new endeavour is to you. So, when I make this commitment to you, it comes from the heart:

'Give me your determination, give me your
action, give me your willingness to learn,
and I will show you the way'

(David Barber)

Leadership Quiz

Can you explain this Introduction to other people? Yes—if you can answer these questions!

1   If you do not have an upline to work with you, with whom should you work? (See 'Get Off To A Flying Start' at the front of the book).

2   What is the relationship between Action, Attitudes and Knowledge? Which is the most important?

3   What does Staying On-Track mean?

4   Draw from memory the diagram of the Four Must-Do Activities for Success. Why are the Four Must-Do Activities so important?

5   What are the two reasons why applying the Six Winning Attitudes is called an 'inner' activity?

6   What does S.T.A.R. stand for in the S.T.A.R. Leadership Programme?

7   What three attributes will make people want to buy from you and learn from you?

8   Why is it called a 'Leadership' Programme when you are only just beginning?

Part I

Winning Attitudes In Action

In Part I of this book I introduce you to four of the Six Winning Attitudes which will drive your business to success.

These four are the personal driving forces, the attitudes which will help you to be the person you need to be to succeed. You will discover:

- *Why you need **Pride** in your business, and how to reinforce your Pride by understanding why network marketing can offer such outstanding rewards*

- *How to develop the **Drive** that will keep you taking effective action in the face of difficulties and distractions*

- *How Drive must be balanced with **Patience** to give time for your business to build*

- *The main difficulties you will have to overcome, so that you can fully appreciate the need for Drive and Patience and prepare yourself for the realities of the business*

- *The importance of developing a **Hunger To Learn**, and how this is achieved.*

Chapter 1

Have Pride In Your Business!

If you are excited, others will be. Be excited by knowing what your opportunity can offer to you and to the people you know. This chapter is to help you Have Pride, one of the Six Winning Attitudes.

The power to transform lives

Make no mistake about it—through your business you have the power to transform the lives of everyone who joins you, but only if you enthuse over it and show Pride in what you are doing. So get excited about what the product and the opportunity can achieve for you, and inspire the people you know with the same sense of excitement!

Now let's see what there is to get excited about and why you should feel proud of being part of this great industry.

Meaningful and rewarding work

One of the most exciting things about network marketing is the satisfaction of the job itself. Doing work we dislike has a corrosive impact on our lives. But network marketeers love what they are doing because they have the seven things that people want most from their work—*freedom, meaning, companionship, the appreciation of others, security, a fair income, and the time to enjoy it.*

Freedom

People dislike having their working lives controlled by others. They dislike taking orders, they dislike having to do things they have not chosen to do, and they dislike the fact that their promotions and pay awards are in the hands of others. Network marketeers, in contrast, have control over their own working lives. They choose when they will work, how much they will work, where they will work and with whom they will work. And they enjoy self-promotion and 'award' themselves their own pay rises, based entirely on results. In short—network marketeers feel free to live the lives *they* want to. *Do you find that attractive? Do you think that other people might find it attractive and want to join you?* And this is just the start of what network marketing can offer.

Meaning

Again, most people feel that their work lacks meaning. The helping professions should offer a deep sense of satisfaction and vocation. But, as any nurse, teacher or social worker will tell you, they feel under-resourced, undervalued, under-paid and under-appreciated. Network marketing can offer the same sense of vocation, but without all the frustrations. You too will experience the deep satisfaction of helping people to solve major and minor problems in their lives and fulfil their true potential. You will see many of the people who join you blossom as they move from poverty and debt to financial independence, from failure to success, from self-doubt to self-confidence, from frustration to fulfilment.

Companionship

Many people lead isolated lives or work with people they dislike. In network marketing, there is spontaneous and im-mediate acceptance of new people. Because of the need to help each other to grow and develop in the business, net-work marketeers forge quick but lasting friendships and you will spend your time with a group of like-minded profes-sional colleagues.

Appreciation

Bosses in traditional organisations are very bad at showing *heartfelt* appreciation of work well done. It is like a great breath of fresh air to come into network marketing where, because you do not *have* to do anything, uplines and corpo-rate teams truly appreciate what you do.

Greater security

Almost more than anything else, we live in a frightened so-ciety. In work, this means the fear of unemployment or bankruptcy, being thrown on the scrap heap in middle age, and the prospect of a long, enforced 'retirement' on a low pension. No matter how hard we work or how good we are at what we do, we no longer control our futures and that makes many of us, at best, feel very insecure. In contrast, to those who Stay On-Track and apply the concept with vigour, network marketing gives security. Unlike most other professions, effective network marketing leaders are *always* in great demand—so even if your present company were to fail you can walk straight into another attractive opportunity.

Open-ended financial returns

As well as the satisfactions of the work itself, network marketing has the potential to offer very high returns on every hour you invest in your business. Top earners achieve an amazing £200 to £300 or even more for every *hour* they work. Part-timers can earn more in ten to fifteen hours per week than they do from their full-time jobs. Part-time incomes of £10,000 to £15,000 per year are perfectly realistic with a good company. Full-time incomes potentially rise from this to a small number of top performers achieving substantial six figure sums—per month!

The time of your life

That said, money is meaningless unless you have the time to use it to do the things you value in life. It is important to understand that in the early stages you will be putting in long hours for little immediate return—you have to *earn* the benefits you will enjoy! But, as your business matures and you develop a group of effective leaders, it will become increasingly possible to take time away *while the business continues to grow without you!*

So, in return for an initial investment of time and effort, network marketing will help you to solve your **ATAC Equation: A**bundant **T**ime to do the things you want to do and **A**bundant **C**ash to do them with. The ATAC Equation is so called because, to solve it, you will need to AT-TACK all the obstacles which get in the way. The ATAC Equation varies enormously from person to person but, in network marketing, you are your own boss so *you* decide what you want to do with your life and how much cash you need to do it. And a good network marketing opportunity offers you the vehicle to achieve the lifestyle you chose.

Freedom, meaning, companionship, the appreciation of others, security, a fair income, and the time to enjoy it—do you find that attractive? *And do you think that others will find it attractive and want to join you?* In fact, can you think of any other opportunity where, in just six months, you can learn everything you need to achieve financial security in a few short years, even if you have no special skills and experience?

But surely all this is just too good to be true? How can network marketing offer all these benefits compared to a conventional business? Unfortunately, there are still many misconceptions about network marketing—and in particular, you will often come across people who wrongly believe that the high rewards are achieved by exploiting customers or distributors in some way. To develop conviction in the worth of your own business, and to help your people develop pride in what they are doing, it is essential that you understand that network marketing achieves these high rewards in a legitimate and very ethical way. How is this achieved? Read the next chapter to find the answers! But first I want to show you...

How to keep your sense of excitement going!

At the moment, you must be feeling excited about your new venture. But, just like a new love affair, that first flush of enthusiasm can go—and you do not want it to! So how do you keep it alive? There are several ways:

- Collect inspiring success stories, write them down and use them to generate a sense of excitement in yourself and in your people

- Use books, tapes and videos to fan your enthusiasm

- Surround yourself with exciting people—go to meetings and talk to successful distributors at all levels of the business

- Above all, get your business going! There is nothing like *Action*, and plenty of it, to get yourself, and *keep* yourself, excited!

Leadership Quiz

Can you explain this chapter to other people? Yes—if you can answer these questions!

1   What power do you have through your business?

2   How can Pride in your business help you to exercise that power?

3   What does ATAC stand for in the ATAC Equation?

4   How do you solve your ATAC Equation?

Answers you should write down and refer to:

a   What seven things would people really like to have from their jobs, but which they hardly ever get and which network marketing can give them?

b   Please elaborate each of these seven things as if you have to explain them to someone you know.

c   In what four ways can you keep your sense of excitement going and growing?

Chapter 2

Why Is This Such A Great Business?

Reinforce your Pride by appreciating why a legitimate and ethical business concept can offer such high rewards.

Three important issues

If you are new to network marketing, you may find it hard to understand how this business can offer so many advantages compared to other business opportunities. Anyone who appreciates how hard it is to succeed with a conventional small business will want to know:

- How can network marketeers earn such high incomes?
- How is it possible for anyone and everyone to succeed?
- How is it possible to build such large groups so quickly?

The answers to these three questions will help you to develop confidence and pride in the network marketing concept, and to understand some of the basic principles of the business.

How can network marketeers earn such high incomes?

People can earn high rewards in network marketing because it is a very *efficient* and *effective* way to sell products and services. And, because it is efficient and effective, it generates high profits which the company can share with those who have helped achieve them. And that's it, period.

Why is the concept so efficient? Network marketing is one of the chains of distribution: the different ways in which a supplier or manufacturer can get their product from their factory or warehouse to the end-consumer (you or me buying it for our own use). The main chains include traditional retailing, mail order and direct selling, of which network marketing is the most modern and fastest growing form. Let's take the most important of these—traditional retailing—and compare it with network marketing:

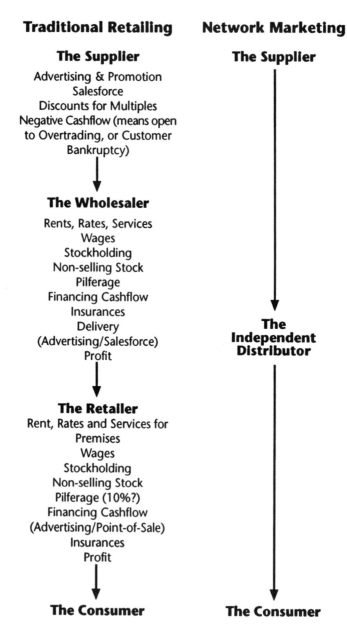

Traditional Retailing   **Network Marketing**

The Supplier   **The Supplier**

Advertising & Promotion
Salesforce
Discounts for Multiples
Negative Cashflow (means open
to Overtrading, or Customer
Bankruptcy)

The Wholesaler

Rents, Rates, Services
Wages
Stockholding
Non-selling Stock
Pilferage
Financing Cashflow
Insurances
Delivery
(Advertising/Salesforce)
Profit

**The
Independent
Distributor**

The Retailer

Rent, Rates and Services for
Premises
Wages
Stockholding
Non-selling Stock
Pilferage (10%?)
Financing Cashflow
(Advertising/Point-of-Sale)
Insurances
Profit

The Consumer   **The Consumer**

All the headings shown under traditional retailing are cost centres which, generally speaking, do *not* occur in network marketing. Since these costs account for between 60% and 90% of the price you pay for a product (net of sales tax, of course), you can now see why it is that network marketeers can earn such high incomes. The chart clearly shows that the high incomes are not the result of a network marketing company inflating the price of the product, as has sometimes been claimed; they come instead from the system 'saving' the costs incurred in the traditional retailing system, and the company re-distributing these very substantial savings to their independent distributors.

Why is the concept so effective? Because network marketing uses the most persuasive sales medium of all, described by David Hunt in his video *Network Marketing* as: '...the *awesome power* of word-of-mouth recommendation'. If you wanted to buy something, who would you be more likely to believe—a professional salesperson or a personal friend?

Also, network marketing is effective because, in an age of impersonal mass marketing, it offers a highly personal, convenient service. Customers can sample and order products at home through people they know and trust.

So don't believe those people who tell you that network marketing is based on high prices or on exploitation—high incomes are earned because good network marketing companies sell outstanding products through one of the most efficient and effective forms of distribution yet devised!

How is it possible for anyone and everyone to succeed?

Anyone who has tried it knows that setting up a normal business is one of the most demanding things you can do. To earn a serious income, you are faced with finding a business idea and managing product development, purchasing, production, marketing, sales, premises, staff, banks, local government 'officiousals', 'uncivil' servants and a multitude of other demanding responsibilities. Despite the hype of the 'enterprise culture', the dream all too often dissolves into stress, over-work and eventual expensive failure.

Even with franchising, which is rightly a heavily promoted way of doing business, you still have some or all of the headaches of staff, vehicles, premises etc. And you still need significant capital and experience, while the potential earnings can be quite modest.

In contrast, network marketing offers all the advantages of a proven success system without the need for capital or for any special talents or experience. This is why it has been called 'The People's Franchise'. And, unlike almost any other way of earning an income, network marketing offers an open-ended earnings potential. How is all this achieved? Because the network marketing company takes on all the worst headaches of operating the business leaving you free to concentrate on the simple tasks of sponsoring, retailing and teaching your people to do the same. And, because everyone is self-employed and home based, capital, premises and staff will never be needed no matter how big you grow.

This has created a business so simple to teach and so inexpensive to start that anyone and everyone is a potential distributor.

How is it possible to build such large groups so quickly?

Conventional companies who use salespeople or distributors give them strictly defined local areas. This places a limit on how much can be earned. But a company using network marketing as its chain of distribution gives you and me the right to sell its product in all the national and international markets in which it is established.

Because the opportunity is easy to duplicate, we can then expand our businesses by introducing or 'sponsoring' other people and teaching them to do the same. They in turn expand their businesses by sponsoring others to do the same, and so on down the levels. Here is a simplified example of how the principle works. If you sponsor just five people and everyone else just happens to do the same, your business will build as follows:

Level	Distributors on this Level	Total In Group
1	You	1
2	5	6
3	25	31
4	125	156
5	625	781

Bear in mind that no one has sponsored more than five people.

You will see that nothing much happens at the start, but then the business explodes. You will also note that, as each level fills up with its full compliment of distributors, you will have more distributors on that one level than the *whole* of your business had before! Just imagine what that might do to your income! Your business will grow by what we call the **Geometric Progression.** This is so important that we will look at it in more detail later but, at this stage, you should simply appreciate that it has awesome power—the power to 'grow' a business at a speed rarely achieved by other types of business.

With all this sponsoring going on, who is doing the selling?

After all, presumably someone has to sell something! Yes. *Retailing is the life-blood of the business* and creates the wealth for all to share. In any reputable network marketing company you will be rewarded *only* on the sales turnover of your group. Any other form of reward may be illegal and opens the door to all kinds of abuse. In return for your efforts in building your group, your company will reward you with a retail discount on all your personal sales, a wholesale discount on the sales of your closest group, and a small but potentially very profitable royalty on the total qualifying turnover of the group as a whole. Build a big enough group, and this royalty will make up 90% or more of your total income, representing around 3% to 6% of group turnover, depending on your company.

As an example of what this might mean, let's look again at the chart above. If all of your 780 people were part-time and averaging only one sale a week each worth, let's say, only £50 per sale, depending on your company this could earn you £5,000 a month! Just one sale each every fortnight would still earn you £30,000 a year! This points up another fundamental principle: *network marketing is a lot of people doing a little bit, not, as in conventional business, a few superstars doing a lot.*

But surely it can't be that easy?

I don't want to mislead you. Network marketing is not as easy to put into practice as this simple overview might suggest—nothing worthwhile in life ever is!

If the Geometric Progression could really run unchecked, you would have the whole population of the country in your business within six months! This is the basis of the common and ill-informed idea that network marketing companies quickly saturate their markets. To prove the point that they do not, I ask at my training sessions whether anyone present actually knows an Amway or a Herbalife distributor (both are successful companies that have been established over ten years in the UK). Very rarely do more than one or two people in ten put up their hands.

In practice, many people coming into the business do minimal or no sponsoring, some will do a little, most want only a part-time business, and only a few will inspire large numbers to join you. The real issue is not saturation, but how to keep the business growing!

Because there are no exclusive territories, many people worry that distributors will be falling over each other in their local area. But, in practice, this is not the case. Remember—you are only showing the business to people you know, and everyone's contacts are different. In fact, far from local distributors seeing each other as competitors, in every network I have ever seen they do the complete opposite and band together to help each other.

Stick to the basics

From this chapter, we can draw four fundamental conclusions about the basics of the business:

1. Word-of-mouth should always be your main approach to sponsoring and retailing. Many companies ban advertising but, even if allowed, it should always be a secondary approach

2. Your success system has to be so simple so it can be 'duplicated' or copied by anyone who joins your downline. This can be achieved through the S.T.A.R. Leadership Programme

> **Simplify to succeed—complicate to fail**

3. You need *Patience*, one of the Six Winning Attitudes, to allow the Geometric Progression time to do its work, which is just another way of saying that success is not instant!

4. Finally, you need to develop *Drive*—the power to keep on going day after day until you succeed...

... and in the next chapter, you will discover how.

Leadership Quiz

Can you explain this chapter to other people? Yes—if you can answer these questions!

1   Someone says that, if distributors can earn so much money, the product must be overpriced. How would you show this is not so?

2   Why is network marketing such an effective way to market products?

3   Why is it possible for anyone and everyone to succeed?

4   How is it possible to create a big group so quickly?

5   Practise until you can draw from memory a chart showing the structure of your business if everyone who joins brings in exactly five people each. Take this down the number of paylevels in your compensation plan.

6   Now work out what happens if everyone brings in six people!

7   Which category of income will eventually make up the vast bulk of your income?

8   A friend says that, surely, the business must saturate. What example will you give them to prove that it does not?

Answers you should write down and refer to:

a   For a distributor, what are the main advantages of network marketing over conventional business?

b   A friend says they cannot understand who is doing the selling. Give them an example, using *your own company's* compensation plan, of what they would earn if their distributors averaged (a) one average sized sale a week and (b) one sale every two weeks, going down the number of paylevels on your compensation plan, and assuming everyone sponsors exactly five people each.

c   What four basics must you stick to?

Chapter 3

Drive—Your Powerhouse To Success!

It is determination plus action which makes things happen. Drive, one of the Six Winning Attitudes: what it is, why you need it, how to develop it and how to put it to work.

Why you need to develop Drive

Lack of Drive is a certain guarantee of failure. Too many people potter along hoping that by some miracle success will come their way. It will not. Nothing is going to happen unless you get out there and make it happen! So let's see how to develop that attitude.

Most successful distributors attribute their success to **Drive**. Drive means **The Bulldozer Mentality** plus **Urgency in Action**

The Bulldozer Mentality means the determination to keep right on going, no matter what. In network marketing, if you Stay On-Track and *keep on going*, eventually you simply must succeed. But, as they say in Las Vegas, you have to be there to win!

A sense of urgency is vital in creating positive action. The stronger your sense of urgency, the more action you will put into your business. Urgency in Action also creates a feeling that things are happening. This encourages people to sign up and stimulates your people to pack their time with activity and quality work.

Drive is what keeps you going in the face of difficulties, doubts and distractions

---

Drive is what takes over after initial enthusiasm wears off. For a time, initial enthusiasm carries most people through almost anything. But, once the honeymoon period is over, there may well be a period of vulnerability. It is common for people to start with immense enthusiasm and then unaccountably disappear with almost no warning: their initial enthusiasm has worn off and they have not replaced it with Drive.

So it is essential for people to build a solid platform of self-motivation in the period before their initial enthusiasm burns out.

There is no substitute for Drive

There is no substitute for determination with Urgency in Action.

Obviously, if you bring personal advantages into your business such as a charismatic personality, good interpersonal skills or relevant contacts and experience, these will help you to succeed—*but only if you understand that they must be additional to, not instead of, your Drive.*

Nor is learning on its own enough: don't confuse learning with doing. As I have said before, the only point of learning is to help you to DO better.

You are on your way to success when you realise that no amount of learning, talent, skills or other advantages will make up for any lack of Drive

---

So how do you develop Drive? By harnessing the power of **Purpose** to the power of **Focus** (one of the Six Winning Attitudes).

Purpose means knowing exactly what you want from your business, and Focus means concentrating your energies on getting it

---

> **Whatever you do in life, you will only
> succeed in proportion to the strength of
> your desire to achieve that aim**

If you focus on a truly inspiring purpose, you will be fired by a sense of urgency, you will bulldoze through any obstacles which block your path, you will want to make every moment really count. The staying power you need to succeed comes not only from concentrating on the day-to-day details of the task in hand but from focusing on what *success* in that task will give you. In other words:

> **Clarify and focus on that which you most
> desire**

This is what gives you the motivation to overcome challenges, doubts and difficulties. Ordinary people achieve great things by applying this major secret:

> **If you constantly focus on your goals, the
> right actions will follow**

This is because they have made success the issue, not the actions. By focusing on the result, they no longer worry whether each action is of itself successful or not; if one action fails, they simply try another. But most of us, by focusing on the actions not on the result we want, make the action the issue. So, if the action fails, we feel a sense of failure.

I know someone who hates public speaking, but she instantly changes this into enthusiasm by taking a photograph of her children on stage with her. She has learnt to focus on what public speaking will do for those she loves, not on the trauma of actually doing it. Bear in mind that, for many people, public speaking is feared more than death itself! This is the practical power of focusing on your purpose.

At some time in our lives we *all* have experienced the power of focus, the power of going all-out for a goal that really excites us. The trouble is that we rarely carry this incredible power into our working lives. But this is something you can change, starting right now, because there is nothing mysterious about developing Drive. It can be learnt like any other good attitude. Become crystal clear about how your network marketing business will help you to get what you *really* want out of life, and then use the simple method I suggest for keeping focused on this inspiration hour by hour. Then your results will come.

Know what you want from your business!

If you are going to stay the course, be clear about what you want from your business: find things which really *excite* you, which really *'turn you on'*! It is only by bringing what you really value into harmony with what you do in daily life that you can be focused, fulfilled and truly effective.

Find goals which really 'turn you on'

What is success? The answer is, 'Anything you want it to be' and that answer becomes your ATAC Equation (see page 20). You may be looking for a modest part-time income or a massive international business—the choice is yours. But, whatever your ATAC Equation, achieving it will be much more certain if you clarify your goals and write them down.

Now, many people have some initial resistance to goal-setting—either they see it as 'American-style hype', or they have tried it before and it did not work. If this has happened to you, it may have been for two reasons: either your goals did not excite you enough or you did not focus on them in the right way. You obviously had some reasons for coming into this business, so your real choice is not whether to set goals or not, it is between having a purpose that is half-formed and woolly, and one that is crystal clear and truly exciting. Which is more likely to inspire you to success?

If you are not comfortable with the exercise I suggest here, by all means develop your own approach: experienced distributors may be able to suggest alternatives and, failing that, there are many excellent books on goal-setting. But, however you go about it, clarify and focus on that which you most desire!

So how do you set about isolating those clear and inspiring goals?

Arrange for some uninterrupted time and sit down by yourself or, even better, with an upline or your co-learner.

Now let your imagination run free—get back in touch with the hope and excitement you felt as a child with all the possibilities of life before you. Don't worry if your dreams seem unattainable; it is more important that you badly want to realise them. If you want them enough, you can achieve them through the vehicle of network marketing. Just look at the successful people in your company—are they doing anything in their businesses that you couldn't do? So don't set artificial limits—seek what you *really* value in life.

Brainstorm the following questions and write down your ideas.

1. What really *excites* you about what your product will do for people?

2. What really *excites* you about what your opportunity will do for people?

3. What could more money or more time bring into your own life that would really *excite* you: relationships, possessions, leisure activities, opportunities for education and self-development...

4. What could more money or more time bring into the lives of those you love and which you would find it really *exciting* to offer: relationships, possessions, leisure activities, opportunities for education and self-development...

5. What could you do with more money or more time to help the causes you cherish in a way that would really *excite* you?

When the flow of ideas comes to an end, go through your list and ask the following question: *Is this really something I want for **my own satisfaction**, or does it come from **other peoples expectations** of what I should achieve in life?*

If it is something which other people expect of you rather than something you want for yourself, cross it out. It will never become a truly motivating goal for you.

Finally, go through each idea and give it a score: 1 for something you would quite like to achieve, to 5 for something you would walk through fire to bring into your life. Then review your '4s' and '5s' and select the two or three goals which really 'turn you on'. Will they bring a sense of purpose to your business? Will they fan the flames of a Burning Desire to succeed? Then they are what you are looking for: a real driving force for your business.

Live with your chosen goals for a few days—do they still have the power to inspire a burning, urgent sense of purpose? If not, you have chosen the wrong ones. Keep looking until you succeed. The more successful you are at this, the quicker and bigger your business will grow.

One final piece of advice: keep your goals private apart from sharing them with your upline or co-learner, and ask them to respect your confidentiality. So many other people have lost touch with their own dreams that they can be cynical and destructive if you attempt to share yours. At this stage of your business your dreams are tender shoots that need protection to grow strong, so don't expose them to the frost of other people's cynicism.

Keep your focus!

Once you have a burning sense of purpose, your next task is to keep focused on your goals, so that you are motivated to overcome every obstacle and put aside every distraction. Like all the best ideas, the way to do this is truly simple—so simple, in fact, that many people do not believe it can work. But I can tell you from my own experience and the experience of thousands of others, that the method I will show you will bring the power of personal focus into your life.

First, capture the essence of your goals in a vivid and inspiring form that you can carry with you on your daily tasks. This is called your **Goals Sheet**. A pocket or handbag-sized index card is ideal or, if this is too small, a sheet of quality paper that can be folded to convenient size. Your goals can be expressed as a short statement, a poem, a diagram, drawings, pictures—whatever you personally find most inspiring. Use your imagination!

Then, at the start of every day, get out your Goals Sheet and renew your sense of excitement. Imagine *vividly* that you have achieved your goals *already*. This is important because your subconscious is very literal. If you see your goals as located in the future, that is where they will stay—in the future. So imagine them as happening *now*! What do you see? What do you hear? What does it feel like?

Finally, most books and trainers recommend that you do this once a day but this is not enough. Do it as often as you can throughout the day. Personally, I like to do this every hour. Perhaps you feel that this is too much, but I find it wonderfully rewarding. It is amazing how distractions fall away and a sense of focus returns! Experiment and find out what works for you.

If you constantly focus on your goals, the right actions will follow

---

Your goals will evolve with time

I strongly recommend that you repeat the goal-setting exercise every six months to keep in touch with your changing circumstances and aspirations. At the start, you may well set quite modest goals—because you may not truly believe that you can achieve more. This is understandable. But, as you get to know successful people within your company and as you see your business begin to grow, you may well find that your deeper dreams begin to surface. So be sure that your goals are dynamic and develop with your business.

Now Take Urgent Action!

Purpose and Focus create Drive. A strong enough Drive will create all-out massive action and that is what you really want!

Urgency in Action does *not* mean that you have to spend more time than you want on the business, it *does* mean that the time you do spend is packed with effective action. Hard work by itself is meaningless, it is effective work that you want. In Part II of this book, you will learn how this is achieved.

People who come into your business will take their cue from you—they will copy what you do, not what you say. If you want them to succeed, you must become the personification of Drive in *action*. So practise what you preach and lead by example.

In the end, action is all that counts

Leadership Quiz

Can you explain this chapter to other people? Yes—if you can answer these questions!

1 What are the two components of Drive?

2 What does a Bulldozer Mentality mean?

3 In what three ways is Urgency in Action important?

4 Drive keeps you going in the face of... what?

5 What does Drive take over from? Why do some people, who start with enormous enthusiasm, suddenly drop out for no apparent reason?

6 Can you name a substitute for Drive?

7 What is the *only* point of learning?

8 Complete this statement: *You are on your way to success when...*

9 How do you develop Drive?

10 What does Purpose mean?

11 What does Focus mean?

12 What limits how far you can succeed?

13 How can focusing on your long-term goals and desires help you to overcome difficulties and setbacks?

14 Remember three episodes in your life when you became totally focused and achieved exciting results. These are important because you can use them to show someone else how Focus pushed you further and can therefore push them further.

15 If a new distributor asked you to define success in network marketing, how would you reply?

16 For what two reasons might goal-setting not have worked for people in the past?

17 How do you know if you have found the right goals?

18 What is your Goals Sheet and how should you use it?

19 Is it better to visualise your goals as something you will achieve in the future, or as something you are experiencing here and now? Why?

20 How often should you repeat the goal-setting exercise? Why?

21 Will the people you sponsor do what you do, or do what you say?

22 In view of this, what must you do?

Chapter 4

Be Patient—Cutting Corners Causes Calamities!

Be Patient is one of the Six Winning Attitudes. Be urgent but not impatient. Give the Geometric Progression time to work. Give yourself time to learn the business.

You need Patience to learn the business

I have been saying that you need urgency to drive your business to success. But urgency is not the same as impatience.

Impatience is a bad thing for a network marketeer because it encourages you to cut corners, not to learn things properly, and to 'skimp' on building solid foundations for your business, with inevitably sad results.

Impatience is also a serious problem when it comes to teaching your people because it makes you put them under pressure to learn at *your* speed. If you force people to try and learn too fast they will actually learn less and you will hinder, not help. Similarly, if someone being shown the business feels under pressure due to your impatience, they are actually less likely to sign up.

A cook will tell you not to put an egg straight into boiling water because it will crack. That is the effect of impatience when you are teaching people in your group or showing the business to potential distributors—they feel under pressure and they crack. But, if you put an egg into cold water and then warm it up gently, it will reach boiling point and stay there for ever without cracking. In other words,

---
You can teach or show anyone anything in network marketing provided you are patient and 'bring them to boiling point' at their own speed

---

Patience is a virtue. It allows you the time to learn the business properly and to lay solid foundations. It allows you to show the business to people at the speed at which they feel comfortable. It allows you to teach your people at the speed at which they feel comfortable.

You need Patience to give the Geometric Progression time to work

Network marketing is called a numbers game and this is one reason: you need large numbers of people selling a little, not a few people doing a lot. This means accepting that it will take time for the number of distributors in your business to build to the point at which they will have a significant effect on your income.

Trying to short-circuit this process by recruiting traditional salespeople or pushing your people to sell more than they want doesn't work, because *95% of potential and existing distributors simply do not want to be salespeople* in the traditional sense. You will only succeed in turning off the great majority and greatly limiting the scope of your business.

The power of the Geometric Progression is a key to the business so we will take a closer look through a very simple example where you sponsor only one person a month and everybody else in your business does the same—not a very difficult target, I am sure you will agree!

In the first four months, your business would grow like this:

Month	IDs at Start		New IDs		Total Group
1	You	+	1	=	2
2	2	+	2	=	4
3	4	+	4	=	8
4	8	+	8	=	16

Sixteen IDs (Independent Distributors) in your business after four months does not sound a lot and, at this stage, distributors who do not understand what is going on may drop out. But, and this is why it is so important that you understand the effect of the Geometric Progression, 'only' sixteen people after four months actually puts you in direct line for a staggering 4,096 after twelve months!

The following chart, which is also based on each ID sponsoring only one person a month, shows you why:

Month	IDs at Start		New IDs		Total Group
1	You	+	1	=	2
2	2	+	2	=	4
3	4	+	4	=	8
4	8	+	8	=	16
5	16	+	16	=	32
6	32	+	32	=	64
7	64	+	64	=	128
8	128	+	128	=	256
9	256	+	256	=	512
10	512	+	512	=	1,024
11	1,024	+	1,024	=	2,048
12	2,048	+	2,048	=	4,096

The four things to note from this are:

1. You have personally sponsored only twelve people

2. No one else has sponsored more than one a month

3. Nothing much happens for a long time (in this case, nine months)

4. After that, it explodes!

Most people would be happy to achieve a group of 4,000 distributors in, say, five years because that should give them a very high income—far in excess of what they could otherwise hope to achieve.

*But if I am only sponsoring one person a month... **what do I do for the rest of the month?***

To achieve that, you and each person in your group need to sponsor only *one* person every *five* months! Here are the figures (rounded):

End of Year	IDs at Start
1	4
2	32
3	128
4	1,024
5	4,096

Please notice again the rules of the Geometric Progression:

1. Not much is required of any distributor

2. Nothing much happens for a while (in this case, for three years)

3. But then it explodes (just look at what happens in the fourth—and, particularly, the fifth—years).

However I should explain that, with such slow business growth in the early years, your business could collapse due to lack of momentum.

One final point to note about the Geometric Progression: very small improvements in your approach to the business can lead to very large improvements in your results. Look at these two examples:

	Business 1	*Business 2*
	Each ID sponsors *5 people per period*	*Each ID sponsors* *6 people per period*
1	1 + 5 = 6	1 + 6 = 7
2	6 + 30 = 36	7 + 42 = 49
3	36 + 180 = 216	49 + 294 = 343
4	216 + 1080 = 1296	343 + 2058 = 2401

So, even if your business seems to be going nowhere, just keep on going. To succeed massively you only have to perform a few percent better than those who fail. And, because anyone can learn the business given time, if you have the Patience and Stay On-Track, you are bound to reach the point where things begin to happen for you.

The sad thing about not understanding the Geometric Progression is that many distributors drop out just before their business would have taken off. So have the Patience to give the Geometric Progression time to work!

You need Patience to cope with drop-outs

As I have said before, the figures in the 'ideal' examples of the Geometric Progression look too good to be true—and they are! As people stream in at one end of your business, drop-outs will pour out at the other. They will leave for all kinds of reasons, some good, some bad, some you can influence, some you cannot.

Here is a picture of what may happen in real life. Of every 100 people you sponsor:

- 75 will do little or nothing
- 15 will do a little retailing
- 9 will become part-time business builders
- 1 will become a full-time business builder.

'We mice understand the Geometric Progression— that's the rate our families grow at!'

The idea that possibly only one person in every ten you sponsor will go on to be an active long-term distributor sounds truly depressing. So why does anyone bother to try and build a business? Because the power of the Geometric Progression is so great that, even with these small numbers sticking at the business, you will eventually experience explosive growth. Don't take my word for it: just look at the successful distributors in your company and you will see that this is true.

Don't become disheartened when people say 'No' to the business. Don't be disheartened when 90% of your distributors fail to get going. Just be Patient and keep working at your business. Network marketing truly is a numbers game. Provided *some people* do sign up, provided *some people* do stick at the business, and provided *you* are continuing to Stay On-Track, sooner or later the incredible power of the Geometric Progression will begin to work for you.

Don't be put off by balloon business-builders

New distributors can be rattled by seeing other distributors achieve incredibly fast build-up rates. If this happens to you, rest assured that it does not mean you are doing anything wrong!

First, although they are new to your company, some of these people are experienced network marketeers. As soon as you learn to do what they are doing (and you should ask them to teach you!) you will be where they are now.

Second, inexperienced people who build fast may well be confusing size with solidity. They are not taking the time to learn the business and to teach their people. But after a few months no one is getting results and their people start to drop out in droves. They make a brilliant start, but the business has no solidity and often disappears as quickly as it grew.

You can make an object the size of a cannonball just by blowing up a balloon. But a balloon has no solidity; it can be destroyed by a pin-prick and deflected by the flimsiest barrier. A cannonball needs more effort to create, but nothing can harm it and it can smash through any obstacle. So don't measure yourself by others. Leading on the first lap does not make a winner. Those people may have had their moment of glory but they have dashed their future hopes.

For you, *this is not a sprint, it is a marathon.*

The only winners are those who cross the finishing line of achieving what they want from life

---

There are no time-limits on success

You can take all the time you need to learn the business. Network marketing has the patience to wait for you to succeed, so make sure your aim is to cross the finishing line.

Build a cannonball business, not a balloon business

Make a promise to yourself that you will stay the course. *The only certain way to fail is if you drop out.*

Leadership Quiz

Can you explain this chapter to other people? Yes—if you can answer these questions!

1 It sounds like a good idea to concentrate on recruiting traditional salespeople and encouraging your people to sell more. Why should you not do this?

2 Someone starts very slowly, and after four months has a group of only eight people. How, by writing out a Geometric Progression, would you prove to them that they should stay in the business?

3 What three things should you explain to your first distributor about the Geometric Progression?

4 Your first distributor comes to you feeling hopeless because two out of every three people sponsored into their business drop out. How do you encourage them?

5 A distributor who started at the same time as you has taken off like a rocket, but you are hardly moving. What, if anything, are you doing wrong?

6 Who are the long-term winners in network marketing?

7 What time limits should you put on your success? Why?

8 What is the one sure way to fail?

Answers you should write down and refer to:

a What are the three main reasons you need Patience? (Hint—review the headings in the chapter.)

Chapter 5

Beware Of The 'Pigs Around The Corner'!

There are certain problems faced by every new distributor. Forewarned is forearmed!

Prepare yourself for the realities of the business

What happens if you drive fast round a blind bend—only to find too late that there is a herd of pigs in the middle of the road? Would the problem be as bad if you knew before you got to the corner that the pigs were there?

Forewarned is forearmed: 'Pigs Around The Corner' are problems which confront almost every distributor. Accept them for what they are, mere obstacles to be negotiated on your way to success, and be ready for them.

So what are the 'Pigs Around The Corner'?:

1. The high drop-out rate

As you may already have guessed, the high drop-out rate is without doubt the number one demoralising factor in network marketing. Distributors who are not warned about this can live in a 'fool's paradise' by assuming that, because they have recruited, say, ten people, they now have the makings of a strong business. But, as you have seen, allowing for drop-outs they are likely to have only one person who will do any real work! It follows that even a group of 100 people may have only ten people in it doing any sponsoring (although there may be more retailers). If you are not warned to expect this, you can end up believing that there must be something wrong with you when a lot of the people you sponsor do little or nothing.

A major purpose of The S.T.A.R. Leadership Programme is to show you how to manage this difficult problem.

2. The need to attract leaders

In most groups, distributors become frustrated because they find it very difficult to recruit charismatic natural leaders. As a result, group growth can be disappointing. Unfortunately, people with true natural leadership qualities are very rare. Top distributors say that, unless you are extremely lucky, you may need a group of 1000 people to find just one! So, if you are expecting them to drop into your lap you should be prepared for a long, frustrating wait. Most groups fail in this strategy and then they are stuck, because they do not know how to create a business in any other way.

There is an answer. A major purpose of The S.T.A.R. Leadership Programme is to show you how to avoid the lottery of finding charismatic leaders by developing effective leaders out of ordinary, motivated downlines. In Part III of this book I will show you how.

3. Friends who 'pour cold water'

I'm not sure a new distributor would like you referring to their friends as 'Pigs Around The Corner'—but they will soon change their mind when someone they know, perhaps a life-partner, best friend or respected relative, pours cold water on the new business they are so excited about!

4. Friends who fail

It is personally upsetting and a big blow to confidence when someone you know well comes into your business and then fails. Human nature being what it is, friends who fail will blame anything but themselves: the product, the company, network marketing, or you, the friend who introduced them to the business. Friends can sometimes be more cruel than strangers!

5. The Emotion Waves

How will you feel when you sign someone up or get an order? I think you can guess—on the crest of a wave! But how will you feel if, on your very next call, you throw away an opportunity by making a complete hash of the presentation? I think you can guess again—pretty awful! You are now in a trough.

He was very depressed,
but hiding it well...

As you work your business, you will experience waves of emotion from great elation to deep depression—perhaps several times a day. Of course, anyone can cope with the 'high' of success but the 'low' of rejection, unless they are expecting it, can make people believe that they are not tough enough for the job. The answer here is to recognise that everyone can be afflicted in the same way and to keep attending group meetings, which will give you support when you are feeling 'down'.

6. The 'Nos'

The inability to cope with rejection is a major cause of dropouts. If distributors got a 'Yes' every time they showed the opportunity or the product, would they give up? Perhaps only out of boredom. If the constant 'Nos' are getting you down, try the following strategies:

a. Understand that this is a sorting business. At this stage, you are only going through the exercise of sorting out the wheat from the chaff—those who are interested from those who are not. The 'Nos' simply go with the territory

b. You are paid only to get decisions from your contacts. Whether that decision is 'Yes' or 'No' does not matter. This is a numbers game; if you approach enough people, enough people will say 'Yes'.

c. Remember that every 'No' has a cash value to you. Let's say that you earn £50 per sale and that you get one sale in five people you approach. Without the 'Nos', you cannot get a 'Yes'. Therefore, each 'No' is worth £10 to you. If you are showing the business, the value of each new distributor will potentially be much greater.

7. The loneliness of self-employment

If you are new to self-employment and used to working with other people, you can be unprepared for long periods of being alone, when corrosive doubts can hit.

The S.T.A.R. Leadership Programme can help enormously because it provides two of the answers:

• To work as much as possible with other people, *and*

• To help them feel part of a team.

8. Contacts who 'no-show' at BOMs or other meetings

It is very common for potential distributors not to turn up for appointments at BOMs (Business Opportunity Meetings) or other meetings. Everyone, but everyone, suffers from this. The culprits can just as easily be people you thought you knew well.

One solution is, where possible, to collect them yourself from their home. Even then, you may arrive to find a house in darkness! It is also wise to phone them the night before to confirm what time you will be meeting.

I'm not a believer in chasing people who 'no-show'. If there was a genuine reason, they would phone you to apologise.

But if you do chase them up, be very diplomatic. You do not want to get a reputation as a pest.

'No-shows' actually do you a favour. Remember that your job is to get decisions and it does not matter if that decision is 'Yes' or 'No'. These people clearly have no motivation for the business. It is better that they save your time now, rather than waste it later.

9. Problems... problems... problems...!

Problems of one sort or another are why people drop out; the list above is just a sample of the most common. It is impossible to achieve success in any field without having to overcome some obstacles. This is a whole subject in itself and I will cover it fully later in The S.T.A.R. Leadership Programme. In the meantime, use the two very successful strategies I have given you already—*first*, preparing for them in advance and, *second*, developing Drive through focusing on an inspiring purpose. Each time you meet a problem, ask yourself the question:

Is my goal worth the effort required to overcome this obstacle?

The difference between success and failure can simply be that one person sees quite clearly what success will bring, another does not. If you learn to see clearly enough what success means for you, you can project yourself into the future and look back to show yourself how worthwhile it was to overcome the obstacle.

Once you learn to look back from the future, you will understand that:

A problem is only a temporary diversion on the road to success, not a barrier

---

Leadership Quiz

Can you explain this chapter to other people? Yes—if you can answer these questions!

1 Why will it help to warn new distributors about the 'Pigs Around The Corner'?

2 Your first downline gets guests who leave him in the lurch by not turning up to BOMs. Another distributor says 'He obviously doesn't have any credibility with the people he meets. I wouldn't waste any more of your time on him'. Do you agree?

3 You get a 'no show' at a BOM. How can he or she possibly be doing you a favour?

Answers you should write down and refer to:

a What are the nine 'Pigs Around The Corner'?

b Coping with 'Nos' is only a matter of getting them into perspective. Show three ways of doing this.

c Give three ways of helping your first distributor to cope with problems.

Chapter 6

How To Reach Your City Of Dreams—Be Hungry To Learn!

Be Hungry To Learn (one of the Six Winning Attitudes). You can learn how to learn. Never assume you know the answer! Take the time and trouble to learn your business properly.

Pride, Drive, Patience, and a Hunger To Learn

Let's pause for a moment to recap. We have seen how you must generate Pride in your business and confidence in the network marketing industry, so that you can attract others to join you. We have seen how you need to develop Drive and Patience so that you can keep going and overcome the inevitable difficulties and disappointments along the way. We have seen that these attitudes can be learnt (indeed, all six of the Winning Attitudes can be learnt). Now it is time to look in more detail at developing a Hunger to Learn. In this chapter we focus on *why*, and in the next chapter I will show you *how*.

Here is a little story that has much to tell you about learning and network marketing:

The City of Dreams

A young couple were passing through the market-place one day when they saw a story-teller with a large crowd around him. Curious, they drifted over to hear what he had to say.

He was speaking of a far away place called the City of Dreams. There, he explained, people would find all their innermost desires and hopes fulfilled.

Now, as it happened, life was being rather unkind to the pair at the time so, when the young woman suggested that they should seek out this city, her companion readily agreed. The story-teller finished and the crowd drifted away, leaving only the two of them and another couple who also wanted to ask the old man the way to the City of Dreams.

'If you keep asking,' he said, 'you will always find people to tell you the way. But,' he cautioned them, 'you must keep asking until you actually reach the gates. *Do not fail to do this because, if you do, I warn you now, you will not reach it.*'

The young man was surprised that only the four of them remained. 'Why is it, story-teller, that with such a paradise to be gained so few of us are setting out on the way? Surely, everyone wants their hopes and dreams fulfilled?'

'Yes. That is true. *Everyone* has dreams and hopes and *everyone* would say that they want those dreams and hopes fulfilled *more than anything else in life.* Had I offered them a magic carpet to take them there, *every single person in that audience* would have climbed aboard. But in reality few people in life will actually *do* anything about it!

'Some, although they would love the rewards, are not prepared to make the sacrifices necessary to complete the journey; others, even though they harbour those wonderful dreams, do not believe that it is possible to achieve them. You are privileged. You are among the few who will set out on that journey but sadly—*although the City of Dreams will be reached by everyone who follows the right road*—even of those who set out, *few will arrive!*'

The group of travellers was confused. 'If all it takes is to follow the right road,' one of them asked, 'how can it be that some will not arrive?'

'Just heed my caution,' was all the story-teller would say. 'Do not stop asking the way until you actually reach the city gates!'

'Well, that's easy!' the other man said. 'It's pretty obvious that we'll have to ask the way—none of us knows how to get there!'

The group decided that the journey would be easier if they travelled together. Along the way, they found that what the story-teller had said was true: everyone they asked knew where the city was, and all agreed that it was a wonderful place, the place they would ideally choose to live—but few would join them on the journey.

Nevertheless, there were a lot of people on the road all looking for the City of Dreams and, after many days, the four rounded a bend and there they saw the wonderful towers and walls of the city rising in the distance, on the far side of a large plain. There was an excited buzz from the throng of travellers as people took off across the plain, hurrying to their destination.

'Come on!' the couple called back to the young man and his companion. But she tugged him back and shouted to the couple: 'Wait! Remember what the story-teller said! Keep asking the way until we reach the city gates!'

'Rubbish!' they called back. 'The way ahead is quite clear! Anyway, the only person to ask is that old man'—they pointed to a farm worker in the nearby fields—'and what can he tell us?' And they turned again to join the hastening crowd.

'I agree with them!' exclaimed the young man. 'Why waste time? That couple seem to know what they are doing and we have travelled all this way together. Besides, no one else is stopping to ask and they can't all be wrong! Let's join the others!'

But still the girl hung back, refusing to move. 'If you go,' she said, 'you go without me! I am going to ask the way.'

The young man realised that she meant what she said. But he did not want to go on without her so he sighed: 'Oh, all right! I suppose we had better go and talk to that old man!' And, with bad grace, the young man hustled the girl over to him.

'Please excuse me!' he said. 'I know this is a foolish question because we can see where we have to get to. But what is the best way to the City of Dreams?'

Instead of pointing across the plain, filled with people hurrying towards the city, the man indicated a large range of mountains to one side. 'The only way is across the tops of those mountains and it's hard going,' he said. 'But don't worry. Take your time. Keep your eyes open and make sure you stay on the route and you'll get there. Everyone does—the only ones who don't make it are those who give up or wander off the track.'

The young man was bemused. 'But why not go across the plain like everyone else?'

'Oh, that!' replied the farm worker. 'There's no way across there! You can't see it from here, but there's a large marsh in the way. A few will stop when they get to it and come back to ask me the way, but most will just blunder on and drown. No, go round by the mountains. It will take you longer and it is much harder work, but you are sure to get there if you persevere.'

The moral of the story—Be Hungry To Learn!

There are many important points for you in this story:

Be teachable! You must keep asking the way. Just like the girl in the story, women are generally more teachable than men. This is one reason why they often make better network marketeers. Just remember:

If people *know* they do not know, they can learn. If people *think* they know, they cannot
---

No matter how experienced you are in other fields, do not assume you know anything about network marketing—ask first.

There are only a few who will do what it takes. Everyone to whom you show your opportunity will have dreams, which they would like more than anything else to fulfil.

But, even if they are attracted by what you are offering, the great majority will not sign up or, if they do, they will do nothing to help themselves, hoping that you will supply a 'magic carpet' to transport them to success. Feel sorry for them, because they are not saying 'No' to your opportunity, they are saying 'No' to their own dreams.

Beware false prophets! The great majority of people will fail because they will not stick to the proven way of doing things. Instead of asking, they insist on going their own way. Act as the young woman did and do not allow them to pull you Off-Track with them.

Be patient! This is a marathon, not a sprint. The only winners are those who enter the city gates to achieve what they want for themselves. You will see many people come and go. Those are the losers because they treated it like a sprint, looked for short-cuts and drowned in the marsh.

Keep On-Track! Of those who Go Off-Track some will come back to you to find the right path, and these have often proved to be the best network marketeers of all, because they have found out the hard way how important it is to stick to the proven way of doing things! But the great majority will sink into the marsh, blaming the company, the product, network marketing, or even you for introducing them.

There are no time-limits to your success! So take the time and patience to make sure you are doing the business right. The proper way to build your business—the way over the mountains—is the quickest way to build your business, but it *looks* as if it will take longer than the short cut over the plain. Network marketing has infinite patience with those who want to learn—it will wait for you to succeed.

But it has no patience at all for those who choose not to learn.

The important thing is not how long it takes to learn, but that you *do* learn

---

Leadership Quiz

Can you explain this chapter to other people? Yes—if you can answer these questions!

1 Can any of the Six Winning Attitudes not be learnt?

2 What attitude makes some people impossible to teach?

3 Should you write-off everyone who goes Off-Track? Why?

4 Your first distributor comes to you troubled because it is taking them a long time to learn. How would you handle this problem?

Answers you should write down and refer to:

a Name the six lessons from the City of Dreams story which are highlighted in this chapter.

b Can you find any other lessons in this story?

c Describe how you would use the *City of Dreams* story to show your first distributor the sorts of problems they will experience.

Chapter 7

How And Where To Learn

Learning unlocks the door to effective action. How to learn. Where to learn. The Training LLAWR.

Why do you need to learn?

Why do so many people fail to ask the way to the City of Dreams, preferring to drown in the marshes of disillusionment and failure? Network marketing is a very simple business, but its very simplicity means that people often genuinely cannot see that there is anything they need to learn.

One of the hardest jobs is to get people to accept that learning has a benefit. Many distributors work hard but, because they have not accepted the right way of doing things, the harder they work the more likely they are to fail. If their business is not building right—and at some point it *will* go wrong—they normally respond by working even harder in the same misguided way. If they don't Get On-Track, they will eventually become frustrated and drop out. Even if you try to tell them, many would rather sink in the marsh than change course. And they do.

Learning the business properly is very important for another reason. I will explain this more fully later, but it is not your own efforts, talents and abilities which will make you successful in network marketing,

---

It is how well the people in your group do the job which will determine your success

---

It is obviously up to you to show them what to do and, if you do not know what to teach them, what odds would you put on your business being successful? So if not for yourself, then for your people, learn how to do the job right.

Focus on the value of learning not the cost

People tend to look at the cost of something but very rarely at its value to them in the longer term. A training meeting, a book, a tape or a video cost only a few pounds but, if you learn something important, their value to you is immense.

But cost is also measured in time and, due to impatience or for other reasons, people often feel that time 'wasted' in learning is better spent in working the business.

> *A young man is walking through the forest when he comes across a woodsman sawing frantically at a giant log. Stopping to rest, the young man notices that, despite all his efforts, the woodsman is making little progress. When the woodsman pauses to mop his streaming brow, the young man enquires: 'Sir, would you not make better progress if you paused to sharpen your saw?' 'Sharpen my saw!' replies the woodsman, 'Where would I find time for luxuries like that? Can't you see I have this great log to cut?'*

Unlike the woodsman, learn to *work smart as well as hard!* In network marketing, the results of learning can be dramatic. A single good idea, multiplied throughout your group, could earn you literally thousands of pounds! Surely this is worth the investment of a few pounds and a few hours a week?

Make learning a continuous habit

If you think about it,

Every situation is a learning situation, but only if you let it be so

---

Every experience can teach you something: if it was handled in the right way, that is how to handle it in future; if it was handled in the wrong way, that is how *not* to handle it in the future.

The only reason so many people fail to learn from every waking moment is because they do not use their eyes to see, their ears to hear or their brains to understand.

```
Menu Today

Baked Barber
Carnegie Consommé
Coddled Clothier
Failla Flan
Kalench Casserole
Roast Robbins
Sautéed Schreiter
```

Be Hungry To Learn—it's fun!

Make your first six months your apprenticeship

This is not too much to ask: most other ways of earning a large income or creating a high-level business require much more commitment! Recognise that no matter how much experience you may have in sales or elsewhere, in this business, you are a newcomer.

Make a commitment to yourself (and to any upline working with you) that you will devote a full six months to learning the business without being concerned about your results in that time—because once you *fully* understand what Staying On-Track means, the results *will* come! And, in network marketing, unlike most other occupations, you earn while you learn! Where else can you learn in a few short months enough to retire in a few short years?

Learn *HOW* to learn

To succeed in network marketing, the *information* you need to learn is relatively straightforward. But there is a right way to pick up new *practical skills*. Here are three simple rules to help you:

Keep trying until you get it right. Any new skill feels awkward at first, and you are going to make mistakes before you get it right. How difficult did it seem when you first tried to ride a bike or drive a car? Did you learn without making any mistakes? But is it all automatic to you now? So don't be put off. Just keep trying for as long as it takes and don't worry about getting it wrong. If it works for others it will work for you, provided you are persistent enough to learn it properly.

Practise and get feedback. Before you apply a new skill in a real situation, have a few dry runs with an upline or your co-learner. Take a colleague along to meetings with your contacts and get feedback afterwards. Without this kind of feedback, it is hard to 'see ourselves as others see us'. Use the 'Learn-Think-Do-Check' cycle: LEARN a little, THINK about how to apply it, DO it, and CHECK that it is working.

The best way to learn is to DO. On their own, no amount of books, tapes, videos and trainings will turn you into a winning network marketeer. You have to put what you learn into action and the more you put it into action, the more quickly you will learn.

Knowledge is never a substitute for action

Where do you find the knowledge you need?

The course syllabus for your six months' apprenticeship is called:

The Training LLAWR
- **L**isten to successful distributors
- **L**isten to tapes
- **A**ttend meetings and trainings
- **W**atch videos
- **R**ead books

These are your five sources of knowledge.

Listen

It sounds obvious but many people haven't understood:

You cannot learn while you are talking

Learning involves listening. God gave us two ears and one mouth, to be used in that order. So to whom should you listen? To *successful* distributors! Virtually all successful distributors will gladly share their knowledge with anyone who asks them.

But you should not listen to *unsuccessful* distributors—they have nothing to teach you. People who fail rarely accept responsibility for their actions, preferring to blame the product, the company, the support they are getting, network marketing, their sponsor—anything. But the opportunity is the same for all. If other people in the company are succeeding then it must be the unsuccessful distributors who are doing something wrong.

Attend meetings

There is a saying in network marketing:

No one ever built a business by not going to meetings

Yet many try. Their argument is, 'I have heard it all before so why go again?' Or they think that meetings are time-wasting excuses for socialising.

So why is it so important to attend meetings?

Meetings are important for learning and for Constant Repetition. Although network marketing is a very simple concept, it is easy to Go Off-Track. The only way you can avoid this is by **Constant Repetition**, and meetings are important for this.

Meetings are places to find Compatible Distributors. **Compatible Distributors** are people who might be useful in your sponsoring activities. It helps if you can introduce contacts to distributors they can identify with because they have something in common: for example because they come from the same background, occupation, ethnic group, age or sex, or have had to overcome the same problem.

At meetings, you might also meet distributors who live some distance away from you. They can be useful for taking contacts of yours who live in their area to a Business Opportunity Meeting if you are unable to get there yourself.

'Tell me, which distributor is compatible with a beer-swilling, raw onion eating, loud-mouthed, pot bellied **ballet dancer?***'*

The technique is to exchange business cards with them. On the back of their card, write their occupation, make a note of their background, estimate their age group and, if it is not obvious from the name on the card, record their sex. You can either file the business cards themselves or create a card index file to keep track of compatible distributors.

Compatible distributors do not need to be in the same group as you. You should help people from other groups and you should be able to rely on them to help you.

Having to go to a Business Opportunity Meeting is an incentive to take a guest. If you commit yourself to go to a meeting a week, this is an incentive to take a guest a week.

Meetings are great ways to re-motivate yourself. All of us get 'low' sometimes! It helps enormously to see and feel action going on at a meeting, and to talk to someone who is bubbling over because their business is going well. At times of doubt or depression, it is important to remind oneself that the business does actually work!

Meetings are great ways to help others. If you want people to be there for you, it is important to be there for them, too:

If you are on a 'downer', you need the meetings but if you are on an 'upper', the meetings need you

---

Meetings strengthen your Pride in your business. Pride is one of the Six Winning Attitudes, and a major way to strengthen it is to go to meetings and trainings, to get inspiration from the success of others.

'They say we will fail if we don't go to meetings—and we can't even get in when we do turn up!'

Meetings are essential for team-building. Network marketing is a team exercise. Some distributors get very jealous of their groups and will not let anyone else near them.

This is not a business for 'going it alone'. If you want to become as successful as possible as quickly as possible, it will help enormously if you tap into the knowledge and help of your uplines and plug that help into the businesses of your downlines. This is what I call **The Figure-of-Eight Attitude:**

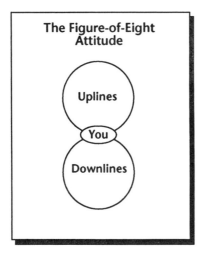

The Figure-of-Eight Attitude

Uplines

You

Downlines

You can see that you are the focal point between your uplines and your downlines, and this puts you in a position of great power. If you are working hard for your uplines, they should work equally hard for you. Your uplines will earn commission or royalty on your efforts, and this *entitles* you to expect their support! So use your power to link up your people with the experience of your uplines. One place to do this is at meetings.

As soon as you have two distributors on board, you should start your own weekly meetings. These are called **Sizzle Sessions** and are important for all the reasons we looked at above. They will help your new people at a critical time early in their businesses when they are most at risk from doubt. If your uplines run sizzle sessions, ask them to help you get going. Otherwise, you will find detailed advice in the third book in the S.T.A.R. Leadership Programme, *How To Lead A Winning Group.*

Listen to tapes, Watch videos and Read books

These make up the rest of the Training LLAWR. Many people rarely read a book nowadays, yet they contain far more information than tapes and videos, and they are much easier to learn from:

- You can go through a book at your own pace
- It is so much easier to refer backwards and forwards in a book than with a tape or video
- You can make a book your own by highlighting useful text and making notes in the margins
- You can use a book anywhere
- Books can cover topics in much more detail than a tape or video.

The fact is that it is very difficult to accumulate enough knowledge just from tapes and videos and you should consider them as *additional* to your reading, not *instead of* it. In fact, tapes and videos are at their most effective as *motivational* tools, not as *teaching* tools.

For daily study, you should develop the **Thirty-Minutes-A-Day-Habit** which means that you should spend at least 30 minutes every day in reading a few pages of a book, listening to a tape or watching a video. Fifteen minutes of this should be spent in going over materials you have studied already, and fifteen minutes should be spent on new materials.

The purpose of The Thirty-Minutes-A-Day-Habit is to:

- Make sure you take in the knowledge you need in easy, 'bite-sized' chunks
- Make sure that even the slowest learner or least experienced person can build a successful group *and teach others to do the same*
- Establish the habit of Constant Repetition.

Constant Repetition is the best way to learn and *remember* what you have learnt. When you start to teach your own people, it means that you will already have acquired the knowledge that you need almost without realising it—because you will have learnt so much by heart! Even more importantly, Constant Repetition is the *only* way to keep yourself and your people On-Track.

Build a library

If you are serious about learning the business, it is essential to build a library of books, tapes and videos covering:

- Your company's opportunity and products
- Network marketing in general
- Personal development.

Personal development is vital and often undervalued. Remember that we placed Attitudes in the centre of the Four Must-Do Activities because they are the driving force for your success. One of the purposes of personal development is to change attitudes. This is important because,

---

You can build a group only to the limit of your personal development

---

So the more you can develop yourself, the bigger and stronger you will build your group.

Some of these materials will be useful to lend to people who are thinking about joining the business and, for this reason, we call these **Sponsoring Aids.** Others are useful to lend to people in your group; these are called **Teaching Aids.**

If there is a recognised supplier in your group, you can get a list of sponsoring and teaching aids from them.

Make sure yours is only a *lending* library. You should only lend, not give, things from your library so make sure you get them back! My workbook *Target Success!* explains this for you, with a recording system already set up to show who has what and when to chase them.

Leadership Quiz

Can you explain this chapter to other people? Yes—if you can answer these questions!

1 What is the danger of the business being so simple?

2 You are working very hard but your business is not going well. What should you do?

3 Your first distributor refuses to spend any money on learning materials. What would you say to them?

4 What stops people from learning?

5 What should your first six months be?

6 What is the course syllabus called and what do its letters stand for?

7 Should you listen to unsuccessful distributors? Why?

8 Draw the Figure-of-Eight Attitude from memory. Why is it important?

9 Why should your uplines put themselves out to help you, provided you are Staying On-Track?

10 What is the best use for tapes and videos?

11 What is the Thirty-Minutes-A-Day Habit?

Answers you should write down and refer to:

a Name three guidelines for learning practical skills.

b Give six reasons for attending meetings.

c There is a big move to using tapes and videos rather than books for learning. Give five reasons why this is a bad idea.

d What three reasons will you give to your first distributor for developing the Thirty-Minutes-A-Day Habit?

e What are the three purposes of Constant Repetition?

Part II
Now Start Your Business!

In Part I you were introduced to the Winning Attitudes you should develop towards yourself and your business. Now, in Part II, let's look at how to put these to work to make your first steps in sponsoring and retailing. Then, in Part III, you discover the secrets of teaching your people what you have learnt.

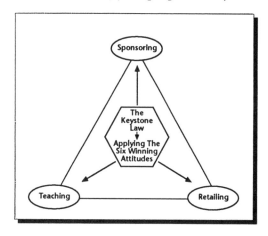

In Part II, you will learn:

- *How to draw up your Contact List and why it is the most important document in your possession*
- *The GUIDE Sequence: the five steps involved in sponsoring people into your business*
- *How to Get-Active—arranging appointments by phone*
- *An easy method for meeting your contacts and showing them the business*
- *The basic arts of retailing your product.*

By the end of this section, you will be ready to begin building your business!

Chapter 8

Your Contact List: The Most Important Document In Your Possession!

Your Warm, Secondary Warm and Cold Markets explained. How to draw up your Contact List. How to categorise your contacts. A 'No' decision is never a final decision! How to follow up people who say 'Maybe' or 'No'.

Who do you have to contact?

An unknown distributor is alleged to have said that if your house catches fire, forget everything else—pets, family, possessions, money, the lot—*but save your Contact List!* Perhaps you need not go quite that far! But the story does illustrate just how important your Contact List will be. A written Contact List is the foundation of your business. It is a fundamental principle of network marketing that:

You *cannot* succeed without a written
Contact List

So who are your contacts? Network marketing is called a **Warm Market** business. Your warm market consists of everyone you have ever met, no matter how little you know them or how long ago. They will come into the following categories:

• Friends

• Relations

• Neighbours

• Acquaintances.

Acquaintances include everyone you know, or have known, who isn't a friend, relation or neighbour; for instance:

- Everyone you have met as a result of work, including bosses and customers
- Neighbours at your previous addresses
- People you met, perhaps socially, at friends, relations and neighbours
- Fellow members of clubs or other institutions, now or in the past
- People you know through your parents and children
- People you were at school with, including teachers
- Regular faces such as the butcher, milkman, grocer, postman, doctor, solicitor, accountant and so on.

People in your **Secondary Warm Market** will also become contacts of yours. These are people introduced or **Referred** to you by your warm market.

The opposite to your warm market is your **Cold Market**. These are people you do not know. To succeed in network marketing, you will not need to contact your cold market.

How should you prepare your Contact List?

When they are preparing their Contact List, new distributors tend to write down only those people who they think, first, would be good to have in their businesses and, second, might be interested anyway. They use it as a selection list. It isn't. Your Contact List is not a *selected* list at all, it is a *complete catalogue*. This means:

Everyone in your warm market should be recorded on your Contact List

---

These four rules of sponsoring explain why:

1. No one can work out BEFOREHAND who will be interested and who will not

If you think you can predict who will be interested you are in for some surprises! You will discover that it is quite impossible to prejudge, so the safest thing is not to try. This leads us onto the second rule:

2. No one can work out BEFOREHAND who will succeed and who will not

Again, you will be amazed how often the 'safe bets' from the people you sponsor do not succeed, but others for whom you had very little hope go on to build successful businesses. So, again, it is quite impossible to *prejudge*, from the people who are interested, who will be worth sponsoring and who will not. This is often the result of the third rule:

3. It is not who YOU know but who THEY know

It is not a person's own attributes which decide whether they will succeed or not, so much as the attributes of the people sponsored into their business. How would you feel if you rejected someone as unsuitable, without realising that they know someone who would have been an absolute winner for you—and then that person was sponsored by someone else? No matter how well you know someone, it is

'Yes, but his uncle is the Duke of Edinburgh!'

unlikely that *you* know everyone *they* do. This leads to the fourth rule:

4. Sod's Law states: 'The one you miss out will be sponsored by someone else and will bring a solid gold big business builder into their business'

Almost every experienced distributor can tell you stories about the ones that 'got away' when they prejudged their contacts and broke these rules. I myself once failed to contact someone who was later sponsored by someone else and would have doubled the size of my business virtually overnight. You can imagine how I felt! The only safe rule to apply is:

If *you* do not approach somebody, someone else will

The *only* reason for leaving someone off your list is when you have good reason to believe that they will not stick to the ethical standards you set for your business.

So, draw up a list of *at least* 100 names, without prejudging anyone. As a prompt, use the headings under 'Warm Market' on pages 74 to 75.

How to categorise your Contact List

This sounds like a contradiction. Having told you not to prejudge, I am now telling you to categorise! So let's make it clear: *the only reason we categorise is because some contacts need to be approached in a different way to others.*

For this purpose, the only two categories we need are:

Executive Contacts:

• Professionals
• Executives, managers and directors
• Salespeople
• High-powered entrepreneurs and businesspeople
• Some people of a high social status or wealthy background.

Non-executive Contacts:

• Smaller entrepreneurs and businesspeople
• Everyone else!

You will find that, generally speaking, your *Executive Contacts* will need a more polished approach. They are more likely to be influenced by the professionalism and business credibility of the person showing the business, and they may ask demanding questions about the technicalities. Your *Non-executive Contacts* are likely to be less concerned by a less polished approach, and are unlikely to ask such difficult questions.

Let me stress again that Executive Contacts are in no sense your 'best' contacts: they just need a different approach. The contacts who turn out best for you will be those who prove to be the most teachable and hungry for success, and they can come from either category.

To make it easy for you, my workbook *Target Success!* has all the necessary forms and instructions to draw up and categorise your Contact List.

In what order should you approach your contacts?

If you are working on your own or with another inexperienced distributor, you should start with your Non-executive Contacts. Start approaching your Executive Contacts only after getting plenty of practice. If you are working with an experienced sponsor or upline, they will decide with you who should be contacted and when.

It makes sense to start locally and work outwards but, in practice, it doesn't always work out like this. What do you do when someone refers their friend who is mad keen but lives at the other end of the country? You should certainly take advantage of opportunities like this, *provided you can support them properly*. As I explain in Part III, for the great majority of people, this means giving practical, face-to-face help. To meet your responsibilities as a sponsor you have three options:

- Work with them yourself on a regular basis, helping them with their phone calls and Two-to-Ones until they are ready to 'fly solo'
- If you can't afford the time or expense, give them to one of your downlines who is in a better position to support them properly (this is called **Stacking**).

- If no one is available, ask your uplines if they can help you out.

If none of these options are possible you will not be doing your contact any favours by sponsoring them, unless they are one of those rare people, a genuinely motivated and confident self-starter.

The early stages of building a national business can involve a lot travel as you work with scattered pockets of distributors. But once these groups mature, you will not have to visit them and you will have more people you can stack under.

When should you remove names from your Contact List?

Only after they are sponsored into your business, or die!

Keep them on your list even if they join another network. People often try two or three opportunities before settling down in one.

'I'm just reading the obituary columns to see if I can cross anyone off my Contact List'

Even if you do not sponsor someone, that does not mean that they may not become a retail customer, or be a source of referrals for you.

But, anyway, sponsoring is always a question of timing. When you first show the business to someone, they may be happy with their lifestyle. So, much as they think it is a wonderful opportunity, it may not be of value to them at that time.

But what happens if three months later their business collapses, or they get made redundant, or they fall out with a new boss, or a member of the family falls ill and they have to pay for home help, or they start an expensive new pastime and need extra money, or their marriage breaks up? Then they could very well become interested in what you have to offer!

**Therefore a 'No' decision can never be
taken as a final decision!**

How to run your Contact Box

Subsequent events may change a 'No' to a 'Yes'—but *only* if you keep in touch. So your Contact List is a vital *follow-up* tool for those who say 'No'. Properly run, you may well find that your initial Contact List provides a significant number of new distributors in your second year, and even more in your third and fourth.

A good approach is to set up a Contact Box, a simple tool for keeping in touch with people on your Contact List who have said 'Maybe' or 'No'. There is not enough room on the main Contact List for recording all the details you need, so cross off their name and transfer it onto a a large-sized index card. You can then note down:

• Their address and phone number

• Their personal and family details

• Dates of all contacts you have with them plus brief notes

• Any other information which will help to make your discussions with them personal.

File your cards alphabetically, one for each contact, in a card index box.

Then phone them regularly sometime between monthly (for someone who may be about to leave, or lose, their job) to perhaps six-monthly (for someone who appears to be happy with their present lifestyle). Use your own judgement and common sense.

During your calls, be careful not to put pressure on your contact. All you have to do is ask them how things are going, and see if they raise any problems that could be solved by your business. If not, after you put the phone down, note the date of your next call in your diary following the guidelines above.

If you do not keep in regular touch with your contacts, if their circumstances change, it will not be *you* who sponsors them, but someone else—and it has happened often!

For more detailed guidance on using the Contact Box, see the next book in the programme, *Breakthrough Sponsoring & Retailing.*

Giving Contact Lists to uplines

No matter how hard people work, their businesses rarely succeed unless *proper* Contact Lists become accepted as an essential business tool. To ensure that this happens, and to ensure that the list is used correctly, you must give a copy of your Contact List to your sponsor or to any upline who is helping you to build your business. Equally, you must get a copy of their Contact List from anyone you sponsor.

This can be a contentious area. You may not be able to accept this advice now but, with experience, you will. You will find that it is a waste of time trying to help a downline unless you have a copy of their list.

Distributors often argue that, as they are going to show the business to everyone they can anyway, why bother with a proper list? In practice, it does not work like this. After a few

'Nos' they quickly become disheartened. The reason is simple: if they have only given you ten names and the first five say 'No', they feel they have already used up half their contacts and are about ready to drop out. If they have given you 100 names and the first five say 'No', they still have 95 to go.

As I have said, you really need at least 100 names but, while you are learning, if you just cannot get someone to give you more than 50, settle for that. If they won't even come up with 50 names, leave them to their own devices: they will never succeed in this business. But leave the door open for them to work with you again as soon as they agree to draw up a proper list.

But be sure to practice what you preach. Distributors often try to get Contact Lists from the people they sponsor even though they have not given a copy of their own list to *their* sponsor. This is very difficult; because you have not done it yourself, why should your people do it for you?

Leadership Quiz

Can you explain this chapter to other people? Yes—if you can answer these questions!

1 How important is your Contact List?

2 What is your secondary warm market and your cold market?

3 What is the single most important message in the four rules of sponsoring?

4 What is the *only* valid reason to leave someone off your Contact List?

5 How many categories of contact are there?

6 In what order should you approach your contacts?

7 Who are your best contacts? Can you say which category they will come from?

8 When should you remove names from your Contact List?

9 Contacts are not just potential distributors. In what two other ways are they valuable to you?

10 'Sponsoring is always a question of timing.' Why?

11 Is 'No' ever a final decision? Why?

12 Apart from being a list of people to contact initially, what is the other use of a Contact List?

13 Explain how you will teach your first distributor to set up and use a Contact Box.

14 Should you work with a distributor who will not give you a copy of their Contact List? Why?

15 Why should you aim for at least 100 names on a Contact List? (Although you can settle for 50 while you are learning)

16 One of the hardest things in network marketing is to get Contact Lists from people. How are you going to explain to your first distributor why you must have one?

Answers you should write down and refer to:

a What four categories of people make up your warm market?

b Explain the four rules of sponsoring to your first distributor.

c Who goes into which category of contact?

d What are the three reasons for categorising contacts?

e What are the three ways of supporting someone at a distance?

Chapter 9

How To Create A Never-Ending Contact List

The Three-Foot Rule. Using the product to interest people in your opportunity through easy ways of retailing. Referrals explained and how to get them.

You need never run out of contacts!

Many new or potential distributors worry that they will not know enough people. In fact, your Contact List should never stop growing. By using just a few simple strategies, you need never get to the end of it!

If you work your business properly, you will only have to find a small proportion of your downline personally, even if you want to build a massive business. The others will be found by the people you bring in, and by the people *they* bring in, and so on down the levels. As your business builds, you will increasingly spend your sponsoring time in helping your people to recruit off *their* Contact Lists, rather than working on your own list. So, to keep your business growing, all you need to do is add a small but steady stream of new people to your Contact List.

There are three main ways of finding new people—by interesting them in the opportunity, by interesting them in the product, or by asking for referrals.

How to interest people through your opportunity

To generate a never-ending stream of new warm contacts, learn to apply the **Three-Foot Rule**. Every time a stranger comes within three feet of you, train yourself to strike up a conversation with them. This takes a bit of getting used to if you are a shy person, but it will come more easily with a little practice. Eventually, you will come to enjoy it!

Once the ice is broken, work the following four questions into the conversation in a natural way:

• Where do you live?
• How do you like it?
• What do you do?
• How do you like it?

Then *listen to what they say*. Just keep them talking by asking more questions in a natural, conversational way. But keep the focus on *them*—their life and their feelings—and not on yourself. If you show interest in people they will find you interesting and you will be amazed how much they will tell you about their hopes and frustrations *provided that you listen with genuine interest*. If you are not genuinely interested in them as a person, but only as a 'prospect', they will quickly spot you as a phoney.

Then, if issues come up that might be solved by your opportunity, simply say: 'I may be able to help you with that. Can I contact you at a convenient time?' You should not try to show the opportunity or the product there and then—make a proper appointment. If you impose your business on people in unsuitable settings you are more likely to put off than to attract, and you will soon lose friends. In any case, a little suspense will make them look forward to your call! So take a business card or a contact number, add their name to your Contact List and get in touch with them later.

You can give the Three-Foot Rule a little help by putting yourself in situations where you will meet new people, by joining classes, clubs, voluntary organisations etc.

How to add to your Contact List through your product

It is sometimes easier to interest people in the product first. Here are some ways to do this as you go about your daily business:

Constantly use the product yourself and let other people see this. This is one reason for the fundamental rule of network marketing:

Distributors must be their own best
customers

Carry your shop with you everywhere. Make your product as visible as you sensibly can, in your home, in your car or about your person—the best ways will vary from product to product, so ask experienced distributors for ideas.

Carry your shop with you everywhere

Get conversations round to your market. Then you can casually say, 'I could have something which might just interest you. Could I come round and show it to you?'

Always look for opportunities relating to your product. With a bit of creative thinking, almost any product can be tied in with all sorts of events happening locally, for instance, fetes, shows, charity events, car boot sales and so on. Put a notice on your stall saying 'DISTRIBUTORS WANTED, PART OR FULL TIME!'. If you are showing at a charity event and your product is suitable for parties, try a sign which says, 'DO YOU WANT TO HELP XYZ CHARITY? PUT ON A PARTY! ALL PROFITS TO THE CAUSE. APPLY HERE'.

How to add to your Contact List through referrals

The third approach is to ask everyone who says 'No' to the product or the opportunity and everyone who buys the product to give you **Referrals**—people they know who would like to take a look at what you are offering.

Let's be honest, for many people getting referrals is far from easy! Unlike some other nationalities, the British are generally reluctant to help. Be happy if one in five or ten people gives you a referral; some people achieve more than this but they are the exception.

But that is no reason not to ask. Remember the Geometric Progression—even these small numbers will make a big difference in the long run. If 100 people on your Contact List decline the opportunity or become customers, you can expect them to give you at least 10 new contacts to add to your warm market with no extra effort on your part. If you have a little group of 50 distributors and you teach them all to get 10 referrals, you have just added a full 500 people to your group's warm market. If one in ten of these people signs up, what is the effect? You have just doubled the size of your business!

Asking people who have said 'No'

It is important to ask for referrals in the right way. Experience shows that instead of asking directly—for instance, 'Do you know anyone who might be interested?'—you will be more successful if you approach the subject indirectly. For example, if you are looking for people who might be interested in the opportunity, ask something like:

- *'Do you know anyone who is not happy with their work?'*
- *'Do you know someone looking for part-time work or an extra income?'*

The same thing applies if you are looking for retail referrals. For example, someone selling lawn-mowers could ask something like:

• *'Do you know anyone with a large lawn?'* or

• *'Do you know any keen gardeners?'*

Asking retail customers

Timing is important when you ask your retail customers for referrals. The time *not* to ask is when you have just got the first order. Instead, ring them up a week or two later and ask them how they are getting on with the product. If they are happy, that is the time to ask for leads. Partly, people may be wary of giving referrals before they have found out if they like the product, but it is also good psychology: your customer is going to be very impressed that you have bothered to keep in touch with them and is therefore much more likely to give you some names!

The need for referrals is a major reason not to pressurise your contacts—if they have not enjoyed their meeting with you, you can hardly expect them to willingly subject their friends to the same experience!

As a matter of courtesy, always ring people back and let them know how things turned out when you got in touch with their contacts. And who knows—they may order some more product or recall another name or two!

Once someone is on your Contact List, the next step is to get in touch with them and take them through the sponsoring process. The rest of Part II will show you how.

Leadership Quiz

Can you explain this chapter to other people? Yes—if you can answer these questions!

1 Why, if you work your business properly, will you need to find only a small proportion of your downlines yourself?

2 What are the three main ways of finding new people?

3 When should you stop adding names to your Contact List?

4 Explain to your first distributor how to apply the Three-Foot Rule.

5 Explain to your first distributor how to get referrals.

6 A new distributor stops asking for referrals because she gets only one from each ten people she asks and she feels that the results are not justifying the embarrassment of all the 'Nos'. How would you convince her that this was a mistake?

7 A new distributor is asking for referrals when they get the order, and is having no luck. What would you advise them to do, and why?

Answers you should write down and refer to:

a Give four ways of adding to your Contact List through the product.

Chapter 10

The Five Steps Of The Sponsoring Process

How not to lose your friends! The sponsoring process can be one area in which distributors Cause Calamities by Cutting Corners! The GUIDE Sequence explained. Ways to Get-Active. What are Productive Distributors? What to do with a new distributor after you have signed them up.

Selling to friends—your worries answered

Now that the moment to contact people you know is almost upon us, let me get some frequently voiced fears out of the way before you actually speak to anyone:

- *'I don't want to put my friends through the embarrassment of saying "No" to me' (which usually means '...put **myself** through the embarrassment of my friends saying "No" to me'!)*

- *'I don't want to lose my friends'*

- *'This means having to sell, and I don't think I'd be very good at it.'*

You may not be worried at the thought of selling but a lot of people are, and it is essential that you learn how to show them that these fears are groundless.

The thought of selling can be quite frightening...

So let's get the story right—no one is expecting you to go 'door-knocking' or to use the Arm-Twister's Sponsoring Kit. Nor are we expecting you to pin your friends and neighbours to the wall until they sign! Instead you simply have to act like a friend, recommending an opportunity and a product which you truly believe will bring something of value into their lives. Do you think you could do that? Of course you could!

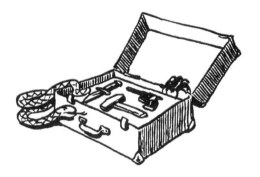

The Arm-Twister's Sponsoring Kit

Because we want you to avoid traditional high-pressure 'selling' at all costs, we never use that word. Instead, we use words like, 'showing', 'sharing', 'inviting' or 'asking' and, where only the product is concerned, 'retailing' to describe what we do.

Sadly, it has to be said that many distributors do try high-pressure techniques and stories are legion of neighbours rushing back indoors or diving behind the garden shed when their local network marketing distributor appears. Believe it or not, distributors have been known to try to sign people up at weddings and funerals! At a less dramatic level, *The Tatler* once reported that you hardly dared to go out for dinner in London for fear that after the coffee your host would whip out a blackboard from behind the curtains and launch into a sales pitch!

Not only does this kind of ill-mannered behaviour give network marketing a bad name, it does not work anyway. What people don't tell you is that these distributors *never* succeed! This is precisely how *not* to do it. All it does is annoy people. It is a betrayal of trust and an excellent way to lose friends! It also ensures that no one will trust you enough to give you the referrals that are essential for the future growth of your business.

Unless you want to become a social outcast, it is essential that you stick to a simple code which is based on nothing more than basic good manners and a little common sense. Approaching people you know and keeping their friendship is governed by the understanding:

> **It is not the asking which offends your friends, it is the pressure. No one minds being asked**

So adopt this Low Pressure Code and teach it to your people:

- Don't try to sponsor in social or work settings. If people show interest, take their number and ring them to arrange a meeting

- It goes without saying, always be open and above board. NEVER mislead people about the true purpose of a meeting. Don't be the kind of person who 'whips out a blackboard from behind the curtains'

- Unless you are very experienced, don't try to retail in social situations—however it can be acceptable in informal situations at work

- If people say 'No', ALWAYS respect their decision and accept it cheerfully. Never chase them or pressurise them to change their minds.

In this chapter I will show you a comfortable, low pressure approach to sponsoring which will have people thanking you for your interest—even if they say 'No' to your proposition. Your reputation for being a caring person to deal with will go before you and, if anything, be enhanced.

'The object is NOT to pin your friends to the wall...'

Provided you are tactful and ethical, there is really no reason to be uncomfortable about doing business with your friends. Until very recent times, most people would trade with people they knew socially—the smith, the doctor, the farmer, the baker and all the other occupations. By bringing trading back inside the local community, network marketing is simply returning to traditional values.

Don't take short cuts: learn to use the GUIDE Sequence

Now that you have drawn up your Contact List and decided who to contact first, what do you do next?

It is common for inexperienced distributors to try to short cut the sponsoring process, even pushing people to sign up at their first meeting. This is like trying to propose marriage on the first date: it doesn't make for a constructive start to your relationship, and you are very likely to be turned down!

If you want to do the job properly, your journey with your contact will take you both along a well-proven path which I have named the **GUIDE Sequence.** This is a series of steps through which you must take every potential distributor if you want to reach the correct conclusion. So, before you get in touch with your first contact, take the time to learn the sponsoring process. But first...

What is the purpose of the sponsoring process?

Contrary to what the great majority of distributors think, *the purpose of the sponsoring process is not to sponsor people!*

Your job is not to get a 'Yes' to the opportunity, it is to get an *informed decision* on it and it does not matter if that decision is 'Yes' or 'No'

You see, we are in the *sorting*, not the *sales*, business.

There are two very clear reasons for this. First, you will spend a great deal of valuable time helping anyone you sponsor, time which you do not want to waste on people who are not really enthusiastic about what they are doing. So it is in everyone's interests that they make the right decisions for themselves as to whether they should become involved or not. This is achieved if you *show* them the business fairly and then help them to make the right decision for themselves, without any pressure from you.

Second, you want them to think well of you so that, even if they say 'No' to the opportunity, they will still feel open to buying your product, giving you referrals, or coming back to you later if their circumstances should change.

That said, you obviously want to show the business well enough so that those people who *should* sign up, do so. We have a saying:

> It is as bad to bring in someone who should
> *not* have come in, as it is to *not* bring in
> someone who *should* have come in

I chose the name 'GUIDE Sequence' because your job is to GUIDE your contacts towards making the right decisions for themselves—and therefore, as we saw, for *you*. The quickest, most efficient way of doing this is to take your contacts through the steps of the GUIDE Sequence:

- **G**et-Active Step
- **U**nfolding Step
- **I**nvestigating Step
- **D**ecision Step
- **E**nsuing Step

Let's take a look at what each involves.

The Get-Active Step

This is the first approach to a contact or potential distributor. As the starting point of the sponsoring process,

> The *only* purpose of the Get-Active Step is
> to lead to a meeting with your contact

The meeting you are trying to arrange is often called a One-to-One.

There are various ways of making that first approach. Choose the one you think will be best for each contact:

1. A phone call inviting the contact direct to a One-to-One

2. A phone call arranging to send a sponsoring aid, which is a book, video or tape designed to show the network mar-

keting concept or your opportunity to a potential distributor

3. A so-called **Fishing Letter** telling your contact about your exciting new venture and advising that you will follow up with a phone call

4. A fishing letter enclosing a sponsoring aid and advising that you will follow up with a phone call.

These options are in order of effectiveness. As a rule, Option 1 is the best and 4 the least effective. But there are exceptions. For example, if you have not seen someone for a very long time, a first approach by fishing letter is sometimes better.

If you phone a contact who does not want to attend a meeting without knowing more, move straight to Option 2 by offering to send them a sponsoring aid.

The technique of actually using the phone deserves a section to itself and is covered in the next chapter.

A fifth way of Getting-Active is to tickle the interest of people you know whenever you run into them, and then follow up with a phone call. Almost as a 'throw away' line, simply say something like, 'I've just got involved in something new. Now's not the time to talk about it, but can I give you a ring later in the week?' Then, having got a 'Yes', *immediately* change the subject. This is usually successful in getting a meeting because it has been so casually done—your contact is expecting a call from you and feels under no pressure.

There is a sixth option for Getting-Active known as **Cold Market Contacting** (contacting people you do not know by advertising, leaflets, phone calls or letters). This is a difficult and risky art and many established network marketing companies do not allow it. Although some talented individuals have made it work for them, it requires specialised skills which are difficult to teach your people. Remember the fundamental principle that network marketing is a word-of-mouth business and you will not go wrong.

The Unfolding Step & The Investigating Step (The U&I Steps)

These two steps run side-by-side. They bridge the gap between the Get-Active Step and the Decision Step.

In these steps, while you *Unfold* your opportunity at a speed at which your contact feels comfortable (thereby avoiding 'Putting an egg straight into boiling water'), your contact *Investigates* it to see whether this is something they should become involved in.

If your contact was sent a sponsoring aid (book, tape or video), these two steps will already have started. If not, they start with a One-to-One. If your company promotes BOMs, ideally these steps would consist of a One-to-One followed by a BOM.

When you have given your contact sufficient information on which to make an informed decision, you then move to...

The Decision Step

Depending on the contact, this would normally take place at or a day or two after the One-to-One, or at or after the BOM, if your company holds these. There are only three possible decisions for a contact to make: 'Yes', 'No', or 'Maybe'. Each requires a different strategy. At this stage, we will only worry about 'Yes'. If you are working with an experienced upline, they will take you through the right procedure for the other two decisions.

If you are not working with an experienced upline and want to learn the strategies for 'No' and 'Maybe' these are covered fully in the next book in the S.T.A.R. Leadership Programme: *Breakthrough Sponsoring & Retailing*. If you feel you have enough to handle at the moment, leave aside the 'No' and 'Maybe' strategies for now, *except that the two actions you must take at this stage with 'Maybes' or 'Nos' are:*

- *Apply no pressure.* Remember that *'No' is never a final decision* and leave the door open for you to go back to them in the future

- *Try to retail the product.* Nothing heavy, just ask the question.

If your contact has said 'Yes' to the opportunity, you move on to the next step of the GUIDE Sequence:

The Ensuing Step

Many distributors think that the sponsoring process stops with their contact signing up. It doesn't, it is only just starting!

The Ensuing Step is in fact the most important part of the sponsoring process and, where a 'Yes' decision is concerned, *by far the longest.* There is no point in signing up people and then leaving them to sink or swim. Otherwise you will, sooner or later, create a situation in which your business just stops growing because your sponsoring efforts are barely making up for your drop-outs.

You cannot call the sponsoring process a success until your new distributor has got a few distributors into their business. This gives us another definition of sponsoring:

The purpose of sponsoring is not to sign up distributors, it is to find **Productive Distributors**

If each distributor signs up two or more people, your group will grow. Therefore:

A productive distributor is one who has signed up at least two people

---

So take advantage of their initial enthusiasm and work closely with them until this has been achieved.

From Productive Distributors, you are looking for **Successful Distributors**. These are people who stay with you and go on to build small or large groups of their own.

If you do not have an experienced upline to help you, take them through the Action Checklist in the 'Get Off To A Flying Start' section at the beginning of this book and you will not go far wrong.

Ban One-to-Ones from your business!

Although we talk about One-to-Ones, two people working together will learn a lot more quickly and do a great deal more than each of you working on your own. Apart from this, working together answers one of the Pigs Around The Corner—the corrosive effect of being on one's own. Even if you are both inexperienced, *1+1 definitely = 5, and possibly more*! If one of you is experienced so much the better.

This means it is a great deal better if distributors always go in pairs to meet contacts. So *ban One-to-Ones from your business*, and from now on concentrate on **Two-to-Ones**! There are two more reasons in favour of Two-to-Ones:

* When you are meeting people you happen to know socially, the presence of a colleague helps to keep the meeting on a businesslike footing. And, while you are new to the business, a more experienced colleague adds credibility to your presentation

* Two-to-Ones reduce the danger of people dropping out. One-to-Ones can be nerve-racking to someone who is not used to them.

It can also be very demoralising for a distributor to get a run of 'Nos'. Two people working together help to give each other the courage to overcome this problem, stimulate each other and keep each other motivated. In fact:

> **There is absolutely nothing to be said in favour of One-to-Ones—use Two-to-Ones instead**

How the GUIDE Sequence gains momentum

When you and your new distributor make the first approaches to people on their Contact List, you are starting the sponsoring process all over again, this time on their behalf. So the GUIDE Sequence is more like a wheel, gathering momentum all the time:

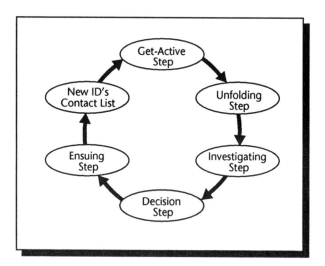

At any one time, you will be working with a flow of people from your Contact List and your downlines' lists at different stages of the GUIDE Sequence.

If we put the GUIDE Sequence into context with the actions I have advised you to take at each Step, it will look like this:

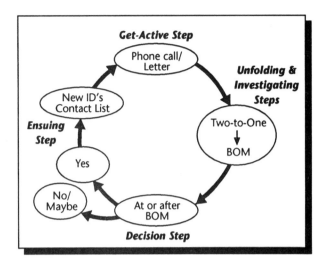

Remember, if your company does not promote BOMs, the Decision Step will take place at or after the Two-to-One.

Nothing happens in the GUIDE Sequence until you Get-Active. We showed you the various ways of doing this above, and the phone call is by far the most important. How you should use the phone in Getting-Active is the subject of the next chapter.

Leadership Quiz

Can you explain this chapter to other people? Yes—if you can answer these questions!

1   Give two very important reasons for not making friends feel under pressure.

2   What is the rule governing selling to friends—or, indeed, to anyone?

3   Someone you meet at a party shows an interest in what you are doing. What should you do, and why?

4   What is network marketing doing by bringing trading back into the community?

5 What is the purpose of the sponsoring process?

6 For what two reasons are you not looking specifically for a 'Yes' decision?

7 But you also want people who *should* say 'Yes', to *say* 'Yes'. What is the maxim governing that?

8 Why is the GUIDE Sequence so called and what does GUIDE stand for?

9 What is the purpose of the Get-Active Step? Is this the only purpose?

10 Which is better, cold market contacting or warm market contacting? Why?

11 What is the purpose of the Unfolding & Investigating (U&I) Steps and what do they involve?

12 The sponsoring process stops at the Decision Step when the contact signs up. True or false, and why?

13 If a contact says 'Yes', which Step of the GUIDE Sequence is the longest? Why?

14 What is a 'Productive' Distributor?

15 How much more quickly will people develop by using Two-to-Ones?

16 Two inexperienced people should definitely not do a Two-to-One together. True or false, and why?

Answers you should write down and refer to:

a What six ways are there of Getting-Active?

b What are the four points of the Low Pressure Code?

c What actions must you take with contacts who say 'No' or 'Maybe'?

d Give six reasons why One-to-Ones should be banned in favour of Two-to-Ones.

Chapter 11

How To Get-Active—Make A Phone Call!

The phone call is the Get-Active Step. The three steps to telephone success. How to overcome fear of the phone, or 'phone phobia'.

(If you are working closely with an experienced upline, ask them if they want you to read this chapter. They may want to get you going with their own approach.)

Three steps to telephone success

You have already learnt that:

The *only* purpose of the Get-Active phone call is to lead to a meeting with your contact, *nothing else*

That meeting is the Two-to-One. In some circumstances, you can invite direct to a BOM, if your company promotes them, but I would not recommend it until you are experienced enough to take this short-cut.

A lot of people are daunted by the idea of making the appointment call. But there really is no need to worry. Trying to sell or even explain the opportunity over the phone does not work. So the most effective calls are simple one minute affairs.

In fact, the less you sound like a conventional salesperson the better. You should sound like a friend or colleague with something important to share. This is not so hard to do, because that is precisely what you are! And then you simply ask for a meeting. There is not a lot to it—just follow these three steps and you will soon be making professional appointment calls:

1. Get Set!

2. Go!

3. Stop!

The Get Set! Step

Keep it short

As a general rule, aim to complete the call in under a minute—the less you say the less can go wrong. Planning your phone calls helps to keep them short and businesslike. It makes the calls easier to do and easier to teach to others.

Talk naturally, using your own words!

Personalise any advice you get on what to say to the way you would normally talk. Script cards and short prompts are a good idea. Adapt them to each situation as you go along.

Oh, shut up!

'Beneficent salutations. I am in attendance to exhibit the multifarious desiderata of a cerebrally stimulating métier.'

Choose your approach

The main decision is to choose the reason you will give for wanting a meeting. You must always *eventually* aim to expose every contact to the business opportunity. But, if your contact is not business minded or you are nervous about showing the business, you may do better with a less direct initial approach. For each call, you have three options to choose from:

1. Showing the product

2. Asking for help and referrals

3. Showing the opportunity.

1. If the call is to show the product

If you are phoning just for a retail sale all you need say is: 'I'm dealing with this great range of products which I think will interest you. When can I come over and show them to you?' (If you know they will be interested in some particular aspect of your product or range, you can lead off with that.) It really is that simple. If you take the other two routes, you have a little more planning to do. The rest of this section deals with options 2 and 3.

2. If the call is to ask for help and referrals

This is useful in the early stages of your business when you approach close friends and family, or colleagues at work. These are the people you might be embarrassed to approach directly with the product or opportunity. So avoid the issue by only asking for their help in finding referrals. With this approach you say something like:

> *'I'm just taking on a new business and I'm looking for people to help me. I am hoping you might know someone who would be interested. Also, I would really value your opinion of the business. Could I come round for a quick meeting to show you what I'm doing?'*

What you must *not* do is break the Low Pressure Code and use asking for help as an excuse to make a 'pitch' on the opportunity or the product. That is unethical and unacceptable. If you are going to ask for help, asking for help is *all* you do. If someone *is* interested for themselves they will let you know without being prompted.

3. If the call is to show the opportunity

If you want to show the business, say something simple like:

- *'I'm involved in a new business with a great product and I think there may be something in it for you. I'd like to come round and show you'*, or

- *'I have just got involved in a new business venture and I need someone to help me to develop it. The potential is very exciting and I thought you might be just the person'*, or

- *'I've just come across a great way to earn some part-time money that I think might suit you. Are you interested?'*

If you can, tailor your comments to the person you are talking to. If you know that the business could offer them something they really value you can make it more personal:

- *You know that yacht you are always dreaming about? Well, I think I may have found a way for you to raise the money!'*, or

- *'Is your job still not working out for you? I think I've got something which might just help you to solve the problem.'*

Tell them you are bringing a business colleague

If you are taking an upline or another distributor to the meeting, don't spring any surprises—get your contact's agreement in advance.

Invite the spouse!

A major reason for people not coming into the business is because they get put off by their spouse or life-partner. They go home fired up with enthusiasm, tell their partner about this great new business, and he or she says, 'Why on earth do you want to get involved with something like *that*?'

The best answer is to encourage your contact to include their spouse in the initial meeting. That way, not only do they get all the facts from the horse's mouth, but it also shows you have nothing to hide.

'Invite the spouse...'

Put their minds at rest, then ask for a meeting

Your request for a business meeting is rather unusual, so your contact may be a little anxious about what they are letting themselves in for. Put their minds at rest by reassuring them that it will be short and sweet. So say something like: 'This is just a quick initial chat to see if you want to take it any further: we will only need around 40 minutes. When would you be free to meet?' Note down the time and place in your diary, and repeat your note back to them to make sure there is no misunderstanding.

Some distributors or trainers advocate that you should make your contacts come to you. This takes a lot more skill and confidence, so I would suggest you meet them at their home until you are more experienced.

If you are going to show a video, check that they have one

You would be surprised at how many people do not have videos, so it is worth investing in a small portable video and TV of your own. If that is not possible, use audio tapes.

This is what it sounds like

All this may sound complicated, but in fact your whole script will only be around 6-8 sentences long and will take about 30 seconds to say:

'Jean, it's David. You know that attic conversion you're saving up for? Well I'm just starting a new business and I might be able to help you to earn some part-time income. Shall I pop over and show you what it's all about? Would you mind if I bring along a colleague who is working closely with me? We will only need about 40 minutes—it's just to let you dip a toe in the water and see if you're interested. Do invite Peter along too if you'd like to—it may well interest him as well. When would you be free to meet?'

Practise... Practise... Practise...

Preparing your scripts is the hardest bit so, before you begin, you should get together with an upline or your co-learner and *practise* until you sound natural and 'off the cuff'. You will save a lot of problems and become good on the phone very quickly. Once you get over the initial embarrassment, practising is fun! It is amazing how your confidence will benefit, because you can practise situations which are far worse than anything you would ever come across in real life.

Get comfortable and in the right surroundings

Setting an atmosphere that is right for *you* will make your calls much easier and more effective.

- Some people like to be laid back and relaxed, so they should get a good, comfortable chair in a quiet corner

- Other people like to feel in control, so they prefer to stand up while they are phoning

- Yet others like to work with a buzz around them, so they might use a family room or a mobile phone in a busy hotel foyer

Use your imagination and find out what works best for you.

Now you are ready to begin!

The Go! Step

With all your preparations, the call itself should be the easy part, even if you do have to pluck up courage. But to help your call go better, try these tips:

Show Conviction and Belief in your voice!

If *you* don't show it, why should they believe it? So remind yourself just before you call—'This is a wonderful opportunity which will transform my life! I really want to share this with them to see if it could help them, too!'

'Conviction and Belief' are not the same as 'enthusiasm'. Unless it comes to you naturally, beware exhortations to be enthusiastic! Many *top-flight* network marketeers who are excellent at making phone appointments sound anything but 'enthusiastic'! It can come across as very false if people try to be enthusiastic when it is alien to them.

But anyone can show Conviction and Belief. All you have to do is to feel strongly inside and then let it come out over the phone.

Smile! Make the call sound personal

A smile comes over the phone very well—the person at the other end gets an immediate feeling of warmth from you.

Many good telephone people find it helps to talk to themselves in a mirror by the phone. This can make the call sound much more personal and intimate—just try it if you don't believe me! If a more formal approach suits you better, you should still work in a 'pleasantly professional' rather than a 'coldly professional' way.

Never say more than you have to!

Remember that you are contacting your warm market and, with people you know, it is almost impossible to avoid saying too much about the business if you spend too long on the phone. As a discipline, have a clock by the phone to remind you to keep it short.

This is nice in theory, but it can be difficult to avoid giving too much information during the call. So you need to have a simple and believable way to avoid getting drawn into details. I recommend that you simply say:

> *'I really can't explain it over the phone—it will be much quicker and easier if you see it. It would only take a few minutes if I popped over with my colleague.'*

If you do get caught saying more than you want to, don't hesitate, don't lie, don't hide the truth!

If you hesitate, it sounds as if you are uncertain or are covering up.

Lying is a complete waste of time because you will be found out as soon as you meet your contact. Your credibility will be destroyed and this is an excellent way to lose friends.

If they ask whether it is network marketing, say: 'Yes' (you have nothing to hide!). Then ask: 'Do you know much about it?' If they are negative, tell them that network marketing is like any other business, some companies are good and others are bad. Yours is one of the top ones around and they might be pleasantly surprised at how good the idea can be. Then go on to say that, leaving the opportunity aside, they may well be interested in the product.

If they still say 'No', stick to the Low Pressure Code: don't get into an argument or try and push it down their throat—you will just create bad feeling. Accept their decision with pleasure because you have got what you wanted—a decision. If their mind is closed, it is their loss! Just thank them for their time and end the call in a pleasant way. You can always go back to them later, after you have proved it works.

If they say 'No' to a meeting, ask for referrals

If your request for a meeting is turned down, ask for referrals, using the techniques you have learnt:

> *'John, I quite understand that you're not looking for anything at the moment, and that's fine. Thanks for giving*

me the time. But do you know anyone who could do with
some part-time income, or who might be looking around in
job terms right now?'

If it is going wrong, end it!

If a phone call starts to go wrong, it takes a very experienced
person to pull it round. Generally, the longer you stay on
the phone, the deeper the pit you dig. So the best thing is to
end it before it gets out of hand. The only problem is how!

**'If it's going wrong:
end it...'**

The answer may be easier than you thought: just tell the
truth! Try something like:

*'I'm very sorry. I am new at this and I seem to be giving you
the wrong impression here. Can I ask a more experienced
colleague to ring you?'*

The Stop! Step

Once you have the appointment, *end the call!* You have
achieved your goal—and if you carry on things can only go
downhill. Don't risk it! Just tell them you have other calls to
make.

How to overcome 'phone phobia'

Even if *you* are confident on the phone, many people are
downright terrified of making these calls and find it the

hardest thing in network marketing. High-level business-people and professionals are just as prone to this as anyone else. Stick to a simple script such as we have discussed, and they will develop confidence much more quickly.

Keep the pressure off by reminding them that this is just a sorting exercise—sorting out the wheat from the chaff, those who are interested from those who are not.

Keep it simple and standard

As you get more confident with the Get-Active phone call, beware of over complication. Most people find that the more elaborate they make the call, the less effective it becomes. And of course it is much more difficult to teach to your people.

The phone call is the Get-Active Step. Until you start to make phone calls, your business cannot even start. The more calls you make, the more people you will get into the sponsoring process.

Leadership Quiz

Can you explain this chapter to other people? Yes—if you can answer these questions!

1 What is the purpose of the Get-Active phone call? Is this the only purpose?

2 What are the three steps of the Get-Active phone call?

3 Your first distributor is terrified of the phone. How will you deal with this?

4 What is the best way to learn how to do Get-Active phone calls?

Answers you should write down and refer to:

a Write down all the stages of the three steps of the Get-Active phone call.

b Now prepare your scripts, based on this chapter.

Chapter 12

Meeting the Contact— Two-to-Ones Made Easy!

The Two-to-One is part of the Unfolding and Investigation Steps. Your contact needs the proper information, properly presented, if you want them to make the best decision for themselves and for you. But you need to present the opportunity with the right conviction: 'This is the best thing for ME since sliced bread, but we are here to see if it is the right thing for YOU'.

(As with the last chapter, if you are working closely with an experienced upline, ask them if they want you to read this chapter. They may have their own approach.)

Be clear about what you are trying to achieve

The purpose of the Two-to-One is going to depend on your circumstances:

If your company holds BOMs, your aim is not to *sell* your opportunity, nor is it to get a decision: *the purpose of the Two-to-One is **only** to invite your contact to a BOM.*

In other words, until you have more experience, you actually do not want your contact to make *any* decision at the Two-to-One—except, of course to go to the BOM.

If your company does not use BOMs, and you are working with experienced uplines but none of them can make the meeting, the aim of the Two-to-One should be to invite your contact to a meeting with an experienced upline.

If there is no experienced upline available, the purpose of the Two-to-One will be to get a decision on the business at the meeting or in the following few days.

All you do is show the business in a simple way

Throughout, remember that you are not here to *sell*, you are only here to *show*. You are in the sorting, not the sales business. The Two-to-One (and the BOM, if relevant) are the second and third parts of the GUIDE Sequence: where you are *Unfolding* the opportunity to your contact to give them enough information to *Investigate* your opportunity for themselves, so that they make an *informed* decision about joining the business.

To do this, keep it all as simple as possible. The simpler you make it, the more likely you are to sponsor someone. If people feel it is easy to copy what you are doing, they are much more likely to sign up. If they feel that it would be difficult for them to do what you do, you will not sign them up.

Also bear in mind that:

The way you show the business to *your* contacts will be the way they will show it to *their* contacts

---

And, of course, the more simply you show it, the easier new distributors will find it to learn and the quicker you can leave them to their own devices and begin to teach the next distributor. Keeping it simple makes life easier for you!

A simple structure for the Two-to-One

Here is a simple structure for the Two-to-One which anyone can follow. There are three stages:

1. Before the meeting
- Practise... Practise... Practise...
- Preparation

2. Unfolding
- Introduction
- Demonstrate the product
- Show the opportunity
- Deal with objections

3. Wrapping up
- Ask if they are interested in taking things further
- If 'Yes', *either* arrange the date for a BOM or a date to meet with your upline *or*, if you have no BOM or upline support, have a detailed discussion about whether they would like to sign up
- (If 'No', ask for a retail sale and referrals)
- Advise about friends
- Get out fast!

Before the meeting

Practise... Practise... Practise...

Just as with your phone calls, you cannot practise too much! It is particularly important to become thoroughly familiar with the products before you attempt to show them to anyone (this is covered in the next chapter).

Preparation

Before you meet your contact, make sure you have everything you need. Is your product in good order and are your demonstration samples ready for action? Check that any videos or tapes you might want to use are wound back to the beginning. When you are in someone's house, the two minutes it takes to rewind a video can seem like two hours! If you are taking your own video or tape machine, check that it is working.

Unfolding

Introduction

Keep this as simple as possible. Don't forget to introduce whoever is with you and explain why they are there. Then say something like:

> *'As I mentioned on the phone, I have just started a new business I am very excited about. (Now spend one to three minutes—no more—in giving your story as to why you got involved. If you do not know the contact, this should include*

a bit about your background. Then continue...) What I'd like to do now is to show you a short video and let you have a look at the products.'

Then, if you are inviting your contact to a BOM:

'As you know, I am very new in the business myself and don't know all the 'ins-and-outs' yet. So then, if you would like to know more, there is a very good meeting on (Tuesday) evening where experienced people will show anyone interested what it is all about far better than I can. It's also a chance to meet some of the other people involved. Does that sound fair?'

That last comment is a good one because it gets your contact's commitment to your plan—and it is very difficult for them to say 'No' when you haven't said anything that isn't fair.

If you are inviting to a meeting with an upline:

'As you know, I am new to the business so, if you like what you see, the next step would be to meet (name of the upline), who is very experienced and is helping me get my business established. As they would also be helping you if you decided to come in, it would be a good idea, wouldn't it, for you to meet them first, before making any decision!'

If you are using neither a BOM nor an upline:

'If you like what you see, then we'll go through it properly in more detail. Then, if you are interested in joining me, we can either go ahead or leave it for a day or so for you to think it over.'

Demonstrate the product

This is the one part which you absolutely must be able to do well. Apart from Practise... Practise... Practise... as I suggested above, experienced distributors will have developed ways of showing the range in effective ways which will make more impact on your contact. You will find some other hints on getting people enthusiastic about the product in the chapter on retailing which follows.

Show the opportunity

With many businesspeople or those looking for a high-level business, you may find it more effective to give them confidence about the concept of network marketing first, before moving specifically onto your company and the product. With people who are less ambitious or business oriented, it is best to show the products first.

When you are showing the opportunity, it is best to keep things simple, and use tapes as much as possible. There are a variety of videos or audio tapes on network marketing in general and most companies offer tapes on their particular opportunity. Don't use more than one in the meeting; so choose the tape you think is most suitable for that particular contact. If your company does not have its own audio or video tapes, use the sales aids which they will supply.

Deal with objections

Why are objections important? Because:

Until you have answered what people do not like about the opportunity, they will not say 'Yes'

This means that you should *welcome* objections and try to make it easy for people to share their doubts with you honestly.

With just a little practise, dealing with objections need hold no fear. One of the reasons for practising Two-to-Ones before doing any live meetings is to find effective answers. But, if you do not know what to say in answer to an objection, don't worry! What you must *not* do is to try to flounder your way through it. Instead, say, 'I'm sorry—I want to make sure I give you the right information on that and I'll need to take advice.'

Then try to phone an experienced upline from the meeting and ask the contact if they would mind talking direct to 'the horse's mouth'. If that fails or is not possible, tell your contact that you will get back to them as soon as possible with the information they need.

If you are taking your contact to a BOM, an option is to say that they will be meeting a top distributor there and, 'I'll make a note to be sure we get that point covered. Will that be OK?' If your contact agrees, this effectively removes the objection as a barrier to going to the BOM. You can use the same approach if you are arranging for them to meet an up-line.

Once you have a bit more experience, you will find more detailed guidance on the art of handling objections in *Breakthrough Sponsoring & Retailing*.

Wrapping up

If you are inviting to a BOM or upline meeting

The low pressure approach to ending the meeting is best: 'Can you see anything in it for you?' or 'Is there anything there that might interest you?'

If you are inviting to a BOM or an upline meeting, if your contact says 'Yes', arrange the details for the appointment.

If the answer is 'No', that's fine! You have done what you wanted to do, which was to show them the opportunity and help them to make an informed decision. Although you ideally do not want them to make the decision till after the BOM or upline meeting, many will decide not to take things any further. Leave it at that because your job is done: *you are not there to get your contact to change their mind.*

If they say 'No' to the opportunity, always try for a retail sale. Again, don't get 'heavy' on this. You have already shown your contact the product, now just offer it to them.

'No!'   *(You are not there to get him to change his mind)*

If they do not want to buy, fine. But you would be amazed at how many sales distributors lose by not asking. Also, see if you can get them to give you one or two referrals. Just casually ask, 'By the way, do you happen to know anyone who may be looking for a part-time or full-time income?'

If you are looking for a decision from the Two-to-One

If you are not inviting to a BOM or to an upline meeting, don't try to get too clever. Again, just ask casually, 'Can you see anything in it for you?' If the answer is 'Yes' or, 'I'd like to know more before deciding', just have an open discussion.

If you told them during the phone call that the meeting would only take around 40 minutes, as I advised you to do, be careful not to overstay your welcome. Before continuing, offer to come back at a later date, if that would be more convenient.

During this enlarged discussion, you will need to cover the following topics:

- Network marketing
- The opportunity, including the teaching and support they will receive
- The product range
- The contact's objections to any of the above.

The teaching and support you should offer are outlined in Chapter 15. This level of support is far more than most distributors will offer and is a very powerful selling point.

There is so much to talk about that it is very easy to drown your contact with information. This just puts people off, so try to stick to the bare bones, saying only just enough to satisfy your contact. In *Breakthrough Sponsoring & Retailing* you will learn how to use a presentation folder to make things easier.

With practise, you will get better. If your contact wants to sign up there and then, sign them up! If not, avoid applying pressure by suggesting that they think about it for a day or two and you will give them a ring to see if they want to take it any further. When you do phone back, again keep it simple. Just ask 'What do you think?' or 'What are your feelings now you have had a chance to think it over?'

Advise about friends

If your contact wants to take things further, you now have the ticklish problem of trying to stop them from discussing what they have just seen with their family and friends, who may have misunderstandings about network marketing and can often put them off.

Don't make this into a big deal or they may think you have a sinister motive! Just say something like:

> *'By the way, **if** you decide to go ahead, you will want to show the product or the business to your friends, so I would suggest you don't discuss this with them at the moment— wait until you know enough to explain things to them properly.*

If they insist on discussing the business with someone, perhaps an adviser, say:

> *'By all means! That's a good idea! But there is quite a lot to discuss and it is important to give them accurate information. Would you like me to see them with you?'*

Of course it is unrealistic to expect your contact not to discuss the business with their spouse or life-partner. Hopefully, as I advised you in the last chapter, their spouse has joined you at the Two-to-One (making it a Two-to-Two). If the partner will not be there, take along good quality leaflets on network marketing and on your opportunity for your contact to show to them. The Insight Network Marketing Library has an excellent leaflet designed to explain network marketing to spouses, friends or professional advisers.

The next step is to GET OUT FAST!

Having achieved your objective for the Two-to-One, the longer you stay the more chance you have of something going wrong—particularly if they have just signed up! You will find it very difficult to avoid saying too much, making it sound complicated, and undoing all the good you have done already.

Get out fast!

But you do not want to make it look as if, having got what you wanted, you cannot wait to get away. As I advised in the last chapter, the best approach is to tell them *beforehand*, when you book the appointment, that you will only be staying for around 40 minutes, and to confirm this again at the start of your meeting. At the end of the meeting, this enables you to look at your watch and say something like: 'I'm afraid we're out of time—we are rather busy this evening, so we'd better get on our way.' Then thank them very much for their time.

Don't be afraid to get your feet wet

No amount of training and practise will make up for actually *doing* Two-to-Ones. The more you do, the easier they will become.

Don't worry about making mistakes: *everyone* does, even the top business-builders. Provided you have kept to the Low Pressure Code, mistakes are nothing to worry about! And don't worry about the outcome either, just do a few Two-to-Ones until you have got used to them. Then the next book in the S.T.A.R. Leadership Programme will show you how to make them even more effective. Improve at your own pace. The important thing is that you *do* learn, *not how long it takes*.

Leadership Quiz

Can you explain this chapter to other people? Yes—if you can answer these questions!

1 Depending on circumstances, there are three different aims for a Two-to-One. What are they?

2 Name three advantages to showing the opportunity to your contacts in a simple way.

3 Why are objections helpful?

4 Inexperienced people react to objections with fear. What should *your* attitude be to objections?

5 What should you do if you do not know the answer to an objection?

6 If a contact says 'No' to the opportunity, what should you do?

7 What is the best way to learn how to do Two-to-Ones?

Answers you should write down and refer to:

a Write down all the steps of the Two-to-One.

b Adapt the advice in this chapter to your own opportunity and product.

Practical exercise:

Practise your Two-to-One.

Chapter 13

Retailing Is Easier Than You Think!

Retailing is the life-blood of the business. Without sales, no one earns anything. But people should retail only as much as they want to, provided that everyone sells SOMETHING.

Keep the pressure off yourself and your customers

Retailing is very easy if you use these basic rules to keep pressure off yourself:

- You are in the sorting, not the sales business. Your job is to show the product to everyone you know, then let them make up their own minds

- Therefore, your job is not to get orders, it is to get a decision and it does not matter if that decision is 'Yes' or 'No'

- The aim of network marketing is to have more friends, not fewer! Stick to the Low Pressure Code on page 92. It is not the asking which offends people, it is the pressure. No one minds being asked.

- If a customer feels pressured by you, they are hardly likely to recommend you to their friends.

There are three levels of retailing, the last of which you should definitely avoid:

- Exposing and Supplying
- Showing
- Traditional Selling.

Exposing and Supplying consists of three very simple steps:

1. Having the product available

2. Making people aware that you have it, *and*

3. Letting them know that you can supply it.

All you do to carry out steps 1 and 2 is to constantly use the product and let other people see this. This is the reason for the rule in network marketing: *Distributors must themselves be users of the product* or, put another way, *Distributors must be their own best customers.* If you are not feeling confident, you should start with Exposing and Supplying, only moving to Showing as your confidence increases.

Showing involves a more active approach. Instead of just leaving the product to sell itself, you positively explain its benefits to the customer while still leaving it to the customer to decide whether it is right for them.

Traditional Selling. The only real difference between Showing and traditional selling is that the salesperson uses a technique called 'Closing'. Closing means making it difficult for the customer to say 'No'. As I hope you understand by now, *this has no place in network marketing.*

The low pressure approach I recommend may lose you the odd sale, but you will get a reputation for friendly and ethical dealing which will be worth far, far more to your business in the long run.

How do you find your customers?

There are four main sources of retail sales:

1. People who say 'No' to the opportunity. If you are working seriously to build your business by sponsoring, you will be spending little time looking for retail sales. So your main source is likely to be people who have said 'No' to the opportunity. Before you wind up the meeting, you should always offer them the product because this is a painless way to build your retail volume.

2. People you approach to buy the product. If you are mainly interested in a small retailing business or you need an immediate income, you may decide to approach people in your warm market with the main aim of making retail sales. And, as we discussed before, even if your main purpose is business-building, it is better to approach some people via retailing rather than making a direct approach on the opportunity.

3. Referrals from satisfied customers. If you are providing the kind of service that builds loyalty, your customers will often be happy to put you in touch with their friends

4. Contacts made at events. Running stalls, displays, raffles etc. at local events, fetes, sales, charity 'dos' and shows.

If you follow the advice in Chapter 9, you should have a steady stream of contacts who, sooner or later, may be keen to see what you have to offer.

Show the product to everyone you know

Where retailing is concerned:

The one sure way not to get an order is not to show the product

---

There are two reasons why a distributor may decide not show a product to a contact:

1. They assume the contact will not want it. This is prejudging. You simply can't tell if you don't ask. Even if they don't want it for themselves *they may know someone who does*, or they may buy it as a present for someone else.

2. They are afraid to make the call. There is no need to feel pressure because you are simply sorting the wheat from the chaff—those who are interested in the product from those who are not. Remember: *It is the pressure that loses friends, not the asking.*

The same rule applies to retailing as to sponsoring:

**If *you* don't show them the product,
someone else *will!***

And you could lose valuable referrals into the bargain.

Even though you call specifically to retail, don't miss the chance to talk about the opportunity. If they like the product, you could then say, 'There is a very interesting business attached to the product. Would you like to know more about it?' Even if they don't come in right away, keep in touch with them because they may well become interested in the long-term. Keep the door open, and many of your satisfied customers will become distributors.

A simple way to show the product

There is no need for gimmicks or tricks. Just share your enthusiasm about the benefits of the product and let your contact decide. But there are a number of simple points you should master as a retail professional.

Become familiar with the product

There are several ways to do this:

- *Personal product use*: your personal testimonial is the very essence of word-of-mouth marketing
- *Company literature*: read and absorb everything the company provides, including label information
- *Practise... Practise... Practise...* practise demonstrating until you are confident. You can never do this too much! Mistakes look bad to the customer and can shatter your confidence
- *Other product users*: talk to distributors and customers about how they use the product and the benefits they have experienced. From this, *draw up a list of all the uses and benefits of the product*, and keep adding to it as you

come across new ones. *Less obvious* benefits can greatly increase your sales. I used to sell a car alarm system to women because its real benefit was to give them a very comforting defensive weapon while they were in the car, not so much because it protected their cars from theft

- *Collect testimonial stories.* Write them down and file them according to the benefit they illustrate. These stories are a powerful way of showing the value of your product to your contacts.

Let the product talk—show it

Most retailers delay too long before giving the customer something concrete to relate to, so the sooner you bring out the product, demonstrate it and let them touch/taste/smell it, the better! I mentioned before that experienced distributors will have found effective ways of showing the range. Adapt these to your own style and personality.

Ask—then listen

Explain to your contact what it is you are selling and then ask them what they are looking for in this type of product. You have one mouth and two ears: use them in that proportion. Spend a few minutes discussing how they would use your product and the benefits they would hope to gain. *Listen* to what they have to say. Most retailers talk too much and listen too little.

As you get more confident, try and tailor your presentation to what you have learnt about the customer's wants. But it is quite OK to use a standard script to begin with.

Features (what a product *is*) are not very interesting. Concentrate on explaining what your product will *do* for them—the *benefits* it will bring them. That interests most people far more!

The rule for sponsoring also applies to retailing:

Until you have answered what people do not like about the product, they will not say 'Yes'

The best way to find out what they do not like is to get them to talk, by asking questions. Treat their questions and objections with respect, and answer them with patience. If possible, tell them a true story of someone who had the same worry but was delighted after they bought the product.

Offer a no-quibble money back guarantee and honour it cheerfully

With most products, it will repay you richly to offer customers your personal, no-quibble, money back guarantee if they are in any way dissatisfied with their purchase. If you have a good product, there is no need to worry about the cost—you will have very few returns (and with many products you can sell any returns at a discount or use them up as samples). But your guarantee will demonstrate your confidence in what you are selling and do wonders for your sales.

Ask for the sale

Although you are being careful not to put pressure on the customer, you *do* have to ask for the sale! Simply say—'What do you think?' If they say 'No', accept their decision cheerfully and ask for referrals (see Chapter 9 for how to do this).

If an order is obviously not forthcoming, an even easier way of closing the meeting is by saying, 'Let me know later if you'd like any of these products and I'll add them to my next order.' This saves your contact the embarrassment of having to say 'No'. It also gets the message across that you are not depending on them for an order and that you are quite relaxed about whether they buy or not.

Let them try before they buy

If people are keen on the product, sell it to them there and then. If they are still hesitating, even after you have explained your guarantee, let them try before they buy. If your product is suitable, offer samples at your own expense. Leave them with the customer—then follow up. For larger products you might be able to leave a demonstration model free of charge. This is called **Puppy Dog Selling** on the theory that, if you leave a puppy dog on trial with someone, they won't want to give it back!

Complete the formalities

To avoid any possible misunderstanding, especially with people who may be good friends, it is best to get your customers to sign the order form. Where possible, you should get money up-front with the order. If you are not comfortable with that, make sure you get cash on delivery. The rule is:

If you *do not* know a customer, never give credit. If you *do*, never give credit!

A true friend will not expect credit. Many distributors have discovered that it is as difficult to get money out of people you *thought* you knew, as it is to get money out of strangers—but a lot more embarrassing!

No sale without AFTER-sale—be proud of your service

Put more dramatically: *Follow-up or foul up!* Decide right now that you will provide your customers with a level of service that will surprise and delight them.

You can make your follow-up service one of the reasons the customer should buy from you, together with the convenience of door-to-door delivery, ordering in comfort at home, immediate personal attention to complaints, 'try before you buy', an outstanding guarantee, you always being available at the end of a phone, and so on.

If the product needs instructions, make sure your customer understands them. If it needs installation or assembly, arrange it. Not only will your customer be impressed and grateful, but you can nip any problems in the bud.

When did *you* last get a call from a salesperson after the sale to see how you were getting on? Yet this is the easiest way to win customer loyalty! So why not contact your customer, say, two weeks after delivery to make sure they are happy and that there are no problems? When you make the sale, note in your diary when you should call back.

There is a saying: *Once a customer, always a customer.* But this is only true if you look after them properly! The whole purpose of *No sale without **after**-sale* is to keep your customers. This should be obvious where products with repeat sales are concerned but distributors often do not realise that, even with 'one-off' products, they will need that customer again for several reasons:

• To get referrals
• The customer might buy another to give as a present
• Your company may launch a new product
• The customer may well need to replace it sometime.

Avoid retail outlets and advertising

Network marketing is a word-of-mouth business and many companies do not allow you to advertise the product or sell to shops. Even if they do, it rarely pays. Most network marketed products do not offer the retailer sufficient profit margin anyway.

How much do you have to sell?

This is not traditional business: *you* decide how much you are going to sell, no one else.

Of course, that works two ways! It also means that, if you want to increase sales through your group, the way *not* to do it is to put pressure on your people to sell more than they want to. *The only way to get more sales is to sponsor more people.*

Do not impose your aspirations on other people

Having said that,

Network marketing is a lot of people doing a little, not a lot of people doing nothing!

It is essential that everyone understands that they *must* sell *something* each week or each month (depending on the product), no matter how big their group grows. If *you* do not get an order this week or month, *why should you expect anyone else in your group to bother?* So set yourself a realistic retailing target and stick to it, and insist that your distributors do the same. But remember—let them set *their own* targets. Any pressure will be counter-productive!

Leadership Quiz

Can you explain this chapter to other people? Yes—if you can answer these questions!

1 What is the maxim governing retailing? Why is retailing important?

2 There are three levels of retailing. Which one should you avoid and why?

3 What are four sources of retail sales?

4 What is the one sure way *not* to get an order?

5 What will happen if you do not show someone the product?

6 Even though the purpose of your call was to retail, what must you also do?

7 What retailing target should you set your first distributor?

Answers you should write down and refer to:

a Your first distributor is nervous about retailing. What can you say to make them feel less pressured?

b What are the three steps of Exposing and Supplying?

c Your first distributor must become familiar with the product. What five ways will you give them to do this?

d What are the eight tips to becoming a retail professional?

e Your first distributor is just getting orders and then leaving their customers to get on with it. How would you explain the importance of *No sale without after-sale*?

Part III

Working With People—
How To Turn Your Knowledge
Into Success

In this final section of the book, we concentrate on two new attitudes and the Keystone Law, which will help you to work well with your people and teach them to Stay On-Track.

- *We begin by exploring in depth the Winning Attitude* ***People Buy People.***

- *I will also introduce you to the **Keystone Law**, the fundamental truth about network marketing which lies behind the Six Winning Attitudes. Understanding and applying the Keystone Law will be the key to your success.*

- *And, as the success of your distributors is what will make* ***you*** *successful, we discover the best ways to teach them.*

- *To close the book, I will show you how to **Have Focus**, one of the Six Winning Attitudes, to ensure the best results for your efforts, and how to set the targets that will get your business off to a winning start!*

Chapter 14

People, Not Products, Promote Prosperity!

*Network marketing is a people business. People Buy
People: one of the Six Winning Attitudes. The network
marketeers' Code of Professional Ethics.*

The people you depend on

The success of your business will depend on how you deal
with three groups of people:

• Potential distributors
• Distributors in your business and in the wider company
• Customers for the product.

Apart from them, two other people are crucial to your success:

• Your spouse or life-partner, if you have one, *and...*
• Yourself!

Unless you relate well to all these people, your business
cannot thrive. This is why it is truly said that:

Network marketing is a people business

Get the support of your life-partner

It is not only the people who are actively involved in your
business who matter. If you have a life-partner who is negative about your business venture you are going to have
problems, as this is a job where the dividing line between
working hours and social hours almost disappears. It is best
not to try to deal with this yourself because, at this stage,
you simply don't know enough about the business. If at all
possible, it is better to ask your partner to meet an experienced distributor. I have done many such meetings and it is

amazing how, when a partner is given a realistic picture of what is involved, their concerns usually disappear.

This is why we try to involve life-partners in the discussions during the sponsoring process, even if they are not going to take an active part in the business.

Just how important are you to your business?

Very, and not just for the reason that it is you, and only you, who can make it all happen. Distributors often make the product or the company the issue. You will soon find from your own experience that this is not true. In your own company some distributors will be enormously successful and others hopelessly unsuccessful, even though they are all offering the *same* product and opportunity. So it cannot be the product or the company which make the difference. If you want to discover the real reason why some people attract so many more new distributors into their business, read on!

Why do potential distributors sign up?

There is a key difference between a successful sponsor and an unsuccessful one: unsuccessful sponsors believe that people will join the network if they like the product or the opportunity. But this is not so:

No matter how good the product and the opportunity, the vast majority of people will not sign up if they don't want to work with the person sponsoring them

---

People Buy People. They will not be attracted to the opportunity unless they are attracted to working with *you*. That is one reason why some people in the same company will build big businesses and others will fail. You will not be all you can be in this business without the Winning Attitude that the most important thing you are offering is *you*. So what will they be looking for in you as a sponsor?

1. That you have great pride in the opportunity you are of-fering (which is made up of the product, the company and network marketing)

2. That you have total conviction in your own success

3. That you make them feel confident that they, too, can succeed and share in your success

4. That they feel confident in your ability, or the ability of your uplines, to show them *how* so succeed.

I hope you feel that sounds easy, because it is! What you do not have to be, I promise, is particularly good at showing the opportunity. I have been privileged to do Two-to-Ones with some top distributors and you would be amazed at how *ordinary* and unremarkable some of them are! But, or-dinary and unremarkable though their approach may be, they *do* make people feel confident in them.

In fact, they make even this apparent weakness work for them; the reaction of a potential distributor to seeing a big business-builder show the business badly may well be: 'I could do a lot better than that!'

Once people have joined your network, your influence be-comes even more important, as you will discover in the next chapter.

The same goes for your retail customers. No matter how good the product, you will not attract loyal customers and regular referrals unless *you* give them outstanding levels of service.

Ethics: the foundation of good relationships

Because your business will rely so much on the trust and goodwill people have for each other, a strong Code of Pro-fessional Ethics is needed for hard business reasons. First, everyone stands to lose if their group or their network gets a bad name with potential distributors and customers. Second, it is in everyone's interests that there is strong co-operation and openness between different groups in a network for trainings, BOMs and other meetings. This means that distributors and groups must seek to co-operate, not compete, with each other. Co-operation is impossible without strong mutual trust.

The guidelines in the Professional Code overleaf are accepted by most top network marketeers as being necessary to provide the foundation for good relationships and preserve everyone's interests. Many of the points in the Code form part of the Direct Selling Association's ethical guidelines and have been adopted by all DSA member companies.

Some points in the Code may need explanation:

Point 1: Sponsoring. 'Poaching' means that one distributor tries to 'steal' a contact who is *already* in discussions with another distributor in same network. Most sensible companies will instantly terminate your contract at the first hint of poaching. It is only a matter of courtesy to support a professional colleague in public, because this is how you would like to be treated if the positions were reversed. You can approach a contact *after* they have turned down another distributor, provided that you are quite sure that all discussions have finished.

Point 4: Guests at meetings who have 'lost' their sponsor. This underlines the point that under no circumstances is it permissible to poach. It is another case of treating others as you would want to be treated yourself; next time, it could be your car that breaks down on the way to a meeting. You would be very grateful to anyone who looks after your guest for you.

Point 5: Other people's Contact Lists. Contacts are the most valuable and sought after resource in a network. If every sponsor is clear that they cannot approach a new

The Network Marketeer's
Code Of Professional Ethics

1. Sponsoring. I will not poach any contact who is already talking to someone in my network. If this happens unintentionally, I will apologise, say that I was not aware that they had been approached and always put in a good word for the other distributor.

2. Social events. I will not 'pitch' at social events. The most I can say is: 'I've just got involved in something which I think may interest you. Can I give you a ring about it?'

I will never hide the fact that a meeting is for business. I will advise guests *beforehand* that a Business Opportunity Meeting *is* business. I will ensure that guests invited to a Party are advised of its purpose *on the invitation*.

3. Hosting. If someone asks me to host a guest or talk to a contact on their behalf (as a Compatible Distributor), I will agree even if the distributor is in a *different* group. I will not poach that contact, *even if they say they would prefer to be sponsored by me.*

4. BOMs, trainings & open events. If I find a 'lost' guest whose sponsor has not arrived, I will either host that guest myself or find a distributor in their group to take over, but I will not poach.

When I assist in BOMs and trainings, I will welcome distributors from other groups and help to ensure that no poaching goes on.

At BOMs I will not abuse the system by sending in my guest while I stay outside to avoid paying an entrance fee.

5. Other people's Contact Lists. I will not approach without a distributor's express permission any person on their Contact List. If a distributor drops out, I will not continue to contact people on their list.

6. If I change networks, I will not 'pitch' distributors in my old network. The most I will do is to advise them of my new network and leave my phone number with them 'in case they would ever like a closer look'.

7. Company politics. I realise that this is a volatile, exciting business and friction between leaders can sometimes occur. Any friction must be kept behind closed doors and away from our groups. The public face, even *inside* the network, must always be harmony and co-operation between leaders. Therefore, I will, if asked, appear as a guest speaker at other leaders' events.

8. Training. By inviting someone into my business I am also accepting a responsibility to teach them provided that they Stay On-Track. The only successful way to teach is to Work With, therefore I am agreeing to Work With them unless they are one of the very rare breed of self-starting achievers.

9. Front-end loading. I will never encourage a new distributor to buy more stock than that legitimately required for samples, personal use and immediate sale. If they wish to hold stocks, I will explain their rights not to have to buy stock until it has been *pre-sold*.

10. Claims of income. All statements I make of potential earnings will be provable and will be *after* payment of downline rebates and *excluding* VAT. I will not state or imply that any level of income is guaranteed, assured or easy to achieve. I will not exaggerate or falsify any part of my opportunity.

11. Other Companies. I accept the principle promoted by the Direct Selling Association that ethical companies and distributors will not criticise other network marketing companies or their distributors, even though they may criticise us.

If the companies themselves and the distributors who supply me are good ambassadors for network marketing and their products do not conflict with mine, I will as much as possible support them as a retail customer if they support me as a retail customer.

12. Active promotion of ethical behaviour. I will promote this and my company's Code of Ethics throughout my business and will seek to stop any of my distributors who do not conduct themselves according to their letter and spirit.

I will be an ambassador for myself, my network, my group, my uplines and for network marketing.

distributor's contacts if they drop out, there is an extra incentive to help them approach as many contacts as possible as soon as they come into the business! Again, this ethic is vital. If distributors are not absolutely confident that their contacts remain exclusively theirs, they will not release copies of their lists to their uplines—and that is essential to the system.

Points 6 and 11: Other networks. Warfare between networks damages both the networks involved, as well as the industry as a whole. These rules are designed to prevent this from occurring.

Point 9: 'Front-end loading' means encouraging a new distributor to buy more stock than they need.

Be vigilant about ethical standards. If you come across a breach of the Code in your group, get it stopped. If you come across breaches in another group, take the matter up with their uplines. This is in your own best interests. Network marketing is one of the few businesses where ethics pays cash in the bank.

Leadership Quiz

Can you explain this chapter to other people? Yes—if you can answer these questions!

1   What is the Winning Attitude covered by this chapter?

2   Which three groups of people are important to your success?

3   Your first distributor is experiencing opposition from their spouse. What would you advise?

4   Why are *you* so important to your business?

5   Your best friend fails in the business and blames you. What will you say to them?

6 In every network, many distributors succeed and many others fail, yet they are all offering the same opportunity and product. What does this teach you about the reason?

7 What makes most potential distributors decide to sign up?

8 How important are the product and the opportunity to your overall success?

9 Your first distributor is losing confidence because they feel they do not show the opportunity very well. How can you turn this to their advantage?

10 Give two reasons why promoting a sound Code of Professional Ethics is essential to your business.

Answers you should write down and refer to:

a If most contacts make their decision on the person sponsoring them, what four things are they looking for in the sponsor?

Chapter 15

The Keystone Law: Your Path To Success Is ONLY Through Your People

The Keystone Law, the fundamental driving force behind your business. The secret of solid, fast growth—Working With. How good you are at Working With does not matter; how much you do, does.

Why is the Keystone Law so vital?

The **Keystone Law** is the fundamental truth behind network marketing which inspires all the Six Winning Attitudes, and your understanding of which will be the key to your success. This vital insight is a wonderfully simple and ethical concept:

> Your path to success is ONLY through your people

As you can see, in our diagram, the Keystone Law is situated at the heart of the Winning Attitudes. A little thought

will show you why it is so important. As you have already seen in Chapter 2, if you are in any way ambitious in this business, your royalties on the turnover of your people will eventually be much greater than anything you could earn through your own retailing efforts alone, and could become *90 to 95%* of your total income! So, unless your goals are very modest, the *only* way to achieve success in network marketing is to help your distributors to succeed and to share in the wealth you create together. If they are not successful, your income will stop at what you, personally can achieve through retailing alone.

This means that the better you understand what the Keystone Law is telling you to do the more you will earn, because the more you will make sure that you are giving your people the guidance they need to be successful.

From now on, never again ask: 'What do *I* need to do to be successful?' Ask instead: 'What do *my people* need to be successful?'

Everything you learn, you must pass onto your people

From this, you can see that *you* do not have to be exceptional at sponsoring or at retailing because the vast bulk of your earnings will come from what your people do, not from what you do.

If you do not have to be an exceptional sponsor or retailer, surely you have to be good at something? Yes, The one thing you *must* be good at is knowing what to teach your people. This is why another maxim applied throughout the industry is:

Network marketing is a *teaching* business and the best teachers build the biggest groups

---

All you can do is to show them the way

As a trainer, all I can do is to show you the way; It is up to you to apply it.

You have exactly the same problem with your people: all *you* can do is to show them the way; it is up to *them* to apply it. So, when it comes to showing your people, you and I are in this together! We have a code of conduct as teachers:

It is *your* responsibility to show people
what to do and how to do it, but it is *their*
responsibility as to what they do with it

If they choose not to follow your path, you must not follow theirs. Very many businesses have collapsed because distributors have allowed their time to be totally taken up by people in their group who were not doing their best to help themselves.

How do you teach the people you sponsor?

If you are working with an experienced upline, they will take the responsibility for teaching your people until you have the confidence to gradually take over for yourself.

If you have no experienced upline available you will have to take the plunge a little sooner. But there is no need to worry. The S.T.A.R. Leadership Programme is designed to help you build a sound foundation.

But, whatever the level of support, the secret is the same. It is very simple, yet very few distributors actually *practise* it, and it is a major reason why they have problems building momentum in their businesses. The secret is simply this:

All you have to do is to **Work With** your
people!

The ONLY truly effective form of teaching is Working With

Working With distributors means going out and doing their Get-Active phone calls with them, doing their Two-to-Ones with them, helping host their guests with them at BOMs (if your company holds them), and taking their contacts through the sponsoring process until they feel confident enough to take over from you.

Network marketeers are very good at *telling* people what to do, but hardly ever *show* them in the field and give them on-the-job support. Advice over the phone, classroom trainings, meetings and newsletters are just not enough on their own! Not only is showing very much better then telling but, if all your new distributors are Worked With closely, they will feel much better supported and are far less likely to drop out.

Again, just as with sponsoring and retailing, *don't worry about how good you are*. It is not being good that counts, it is doing it. Working With people badly is *far* better than not Working With them at all. Two people working badly together *will* learn a lot more quickly, *will* get results—and will certainly get results *very* much more quickly than each trying on their own. In fact, their results will be at least *five times* better.

Once you are doing enough sponsoring, retailing and Working With then, of course, the better you are the quicker your business will grow. But, when people talk about being 'bad' and 'good', they think in terms of success and failure and that is not true: it may effect your *rate* of growth but not your eventual success. It is true that some people need to do more than others to get the same results, but that is all. No matter how 'bad' you are at any of these activities, if you do enough of them, you *will* succeed, although it may take you longer.

This wonderful business is very forgiving *provided* you stick to its rules. It says, 'Learn the simple basics of sponsoring, retailing, and Working With, do enough of them and *stick to them'*. It does not add, 'And you have to be exceptional at them'.

Don't rely on charisma

Having stressed the importance of Working With, it will not take you long to discover that many successful distributors have built large businesses without Working With their distributors. It *is* possible to earn top money with the attitude of bringing people in and then letting them get on with it on their own.

The trouble is that, without exception, only those with *charisma* can achieve this. Whatever they do in life, they will succeed because people with charisma are the natural leaders. Like pied pipers, whatever tune they play, people will follow. Where network marketing is concerned, the power of their sponsoring skills and their ability to motivate large groups means that they can keep their group momentum going on the strength of their personalities alone.

However, even they, massively successful though they are, would have built far bigger groups more quickly, and with much less effort, had they understood the importance of Working With their people in the field.

True charisma is such a rare quality that you may have to bring many hundreds of new distributors into your business to find just one natural downline leader. If you don't want to leave your success to luck, you must learn how to achieve results with ordinary people. And that is where the mass of your growth will come from.

With the S.T.A.R. Leadership Programme, you can build a successful business *whether you have charisma or not.* If you teach your people to Work With the people *they* bring into the business,

---

You can now show any one of your people how to build a successful group, whether they are natural leaders or not

---

But I personally believe that there is a deeper, ethical reason for Working With the people you sponsor. Although it is good business sense, I believe that the overriding reason is:

If you encourage people to join your business, do you not also have the moral responsibility to give them all the support they need to succeed?

But do you have to Work With everyone?

No. Work only with those who are willing to Get On-Track and Stay On-Track. If you do anything else, you will be taken for a ride! Many people, while doing almost nothing to build their businesses, will graciously allow *you* to work your backside off for them! The rule is:

Work *With* people, but never work *instead* of them

On the basis of what we have learnt since, let's now update the definition of On-Track which I gave on page 8.

Someone is On-Track if they are:

- Putting in the time and the effort they promised

- Willing to Work With you and learn from you, *and*

- Willing to *apply* what you discuss with the right attitudes, particularly Drive and Focus.

If they are On-track, you owe a responsibility to work very hard with them. And it will *pay* you to work very hard with them.

If they Go Off-Track, in other words:

- If they do not put in the time and effort they promised, *or*
- If they are not willing to learn or to Work With you, *or*
- If they do not apply what they have learnt with the right attitudes, particularly Drive and Focus...

...then it is time to either spend more time with someone else who has earned your loyalty by Staying On-Track or to sponsor new distributors.

Trying to help people who are not helping themselves will affect the health of your whole group. The Theory of Duplication is the subject of the next chapter. According to this theory, if you Work With people who are Off-Track, you are teaching your people the same bad habit. The answer is to create good habits in your group by only Working With people who are On-Track.

Leadership Quiz

Can you explain this chapter to other people? Yes—if you can answer these questions!

1   Explain to your first distributor why the Keystone Law is so important.

2   Your first distributor asks you, 'What can I do to make myself more successful?' What would you reply?

3   What is your code of conduct as a teacher?

4   What is the most effective form of teaching?

5   What does Working With actually mean in practice?

6   One of your distributors feels they are not good enough to Work With their people. What will you say to them?

7 You and your most active downlines are ambitious to build a big group as fast as possible The trouble is that none of you are natural, charismatic leaders. What are you going to do about it?

8 How do you decide who to Work With and who not to?

9 What is the new definition of On-Track?

10 If you Work With the wrong people, what are you teaching your group to do?

Answers you should write down and refer to:

a You are going to give a presentation to your group about the importance of Working With. What would you say?

Chapter 16

The Theory Of Duplication: The Basis Of All Successful Teaching

You will often hear people saying, 'It must be easily Duplicatable'. What does this mean?

Your actions set the tone for your whole group

It must be easily Duplicatable means that your group is going to take its lead from you and copy or 'duplicate' whatever you do. Your teaching, and the way you do things, is going to be copied or 'duplicated' down your network, whether you like it or not.

The **Theory of Duplication** states:

1. People tend to do things in very much the same way as they were taught themselves

2. People tend to teach others in very much the same way as they were taught themselves

3. People will copy what you do, not do what you say

4. Bad habits Duplicate more easily than good ones

5. Bad habits arrive unnoticed but depart with great reluctance. It is easier to change a good habit to a bad one, than a bad habit to a good one.

Bad habits are easy to form and hard to change

This instinct for duplication is so strong that people will still give in to it even if they *know* the lesson is a bad one. As is well known, people who have suffered at the hands of alcoholic or abusing parents, far from making sure that they avoid the same mistakes, are in fact much more likely to repeat these behaviours themselves in adult life.

The same applies in network marketing. If you have bad habits, your group will copy you. Just reflect on what this means: the mind boggles at the thought of 100 or 1,000 people copying your bad habits! Is that really what you want?

To compound the problem, human beings find it easier to develop bad habits than good ones. We all know that it is easy to lose a good habit but that once a bad habit has formed, it can be depressingly difficult to change.

So you will need to be constantly vigilant and you must teach your people to be the same, because once bad habits get into your group they will spread like wildfire and be incredibly difficult to change. Keeping good habits going (in other words, Keeping On-Track) means Constant Repetition of the basic lessons and this is one reason why meetings are so important.

As you can see, the maxim, common in conventional organisations, of *do what I say, not what I do,* will not work if you apply it in your business. There are many examples of this. The distributors who have the worst problem in getting Contact Lists from their people are the ones who did not give one to their sponsors. The people who have the worst problem in getting their distributors to contact *everyone* in their warm market are those who have not done it themselves. And so on.

Understanding Duplication is a key to *all* successful teaching in network marketing. It is therefore a key to a strong network

---

Get your training right from day one

Rule 5, *It is easier to change a good habit to a bad one, than a bad habit to a good one,* makes it very important to introduce good habits at the start, and *start as you mean to go on.*

The S.T.A.R. Leadership Programme is a teaching tool which will enable you to establish good habits in your group from the start. It will spare you the agonies I have seen countless distributors suffer as they struggle, often unsuccessfully, to change bad work habits in their group into good ones. These unfortunate people are often only copying their uplines' mistakes, which is just what the Theory of Duplication predicts.

The most important lesson for you to Duplicate is that in the long term, *how* to do a job is less important than developing the right *attitudes* to doing it. Attitude is always the key to everything. Attitude is far more important than technique. No matter how perfect the technique, if it is not backed up by the right attitudes, success will not follow. But the right attitudes will overcome all sorts of problems in technique.

Leadership Quiz

Can you explain this chapter to other people? Yes—if you can answer these questions!

1 What does 'Duplicatable' mean?

2 Will people copy a habit even if they know it is a bad one?

3 Which habits Duplicate more easily—bad ones or good ones?

4 Is it easier to replace a good habit with a bad one, or a bad habit with a good one?

5 What is the best way to keep good habits going?

6 Why is the Theory of Duplication so important to you?

7 Which is more important in the long run, your *technical skill* at doing a job, or the *attitudes* behind doing that job?

Answers you should write down and refer to:

a Write out the Theory of Duplication.

Chapter 17

The Power Of Focus

*How to focus on the actions that will bring you success.
The two types of focus: on the outward Must-Do Activities,
and on the purposes that are driving your business.*

The first type of focus: on the outward Must-Do Activities

There are two different aspects to the Winning Attitude of **Have Focus**. The first is designed to focus your attitudes in the right way on the three *outward* Must-Do Activities of Sponsoring, Retailing and Teaching. These are:

- **Sponsoring:** *Sponsor... Sponsor... Sponsor*
- **Retailing:** *Retailing is the lifeblood of the business—no retailing, no blood*
- **Teaching:** *This is a teaching business.*

Sponsor... Sponsor... Sponsor

Without sponsoring, nothing happens. Without watering, your garden will die; without continuous sponsoring, your group will also wither and die. The only difference is that, in business-building, there are no seasons! Keep watering and your plants will keep blooming.

Every upline will tell you that it is important to put heavy activity behind your sponsoring effort. *Sponsor... Sponsor... Sponsor...* People often take this to mean that you should spend your time sponsoring on your own account rather than helping your downlines to build their businesses. But this is a serious misunderstanding. Yes, you must *Sponsor... Sponsor... Sponsor...*, that is the basis of all successful business-building, *but it does not have to be from your own Contact List.*

So long as you get new distributors coming into your business, does it matter whether they are off your Contact List or off the Contact List of a downline? No! Either way your business is growing.

The difference is that, if you help a new distributor to bring in someone off *their* Contact List (rather than both of you working on your own, which is usually what happens) and both of you help the new person to do the same, then:

1. Your business will grow more quickly

2. It will grow with a stronger foundation because everyone is helping everyone else

3. You will reduce the drop-out rate because people are very much more likely to keep going if they are Working With someone else

4. Even your successful people will be more successful, more quickly.

Retailing is the lifeblood of the business—no retailing, no blood

If nothing happens when no one sponsors, no one earns if no one retails! You cannot, in network marketing, make people retail more than they want to. What you can do is expect everyone to retail *something* every month—and by that I mean sell something to people outside the network, not buying just for their own consumption.

You can also expect people to become users of the product—what right have they to recommend the product to others if they do not use it themselves? And for companies with more than one product, they should use the whole range, within reason: men don't have to use perfumes, for example! Of course, they *should* say that, if they were to use such a product, this is the one they would choose!

You can also expect members of their immediate family to be users of the product.

'Did you say ... no retailing ... no BLOOD?!!

This is a teaching business

Teaching is the only way to apply the Keystone Law. As we saw in the last chapter, if you are going to be serious about supporting your people and applying the Keystone Law, the only real way is to Work With them.

The second type of focus: harnessing the power of purpose

The second point of Have Focus is to focus your activities on three other important foundations of success:

- Structure = Security
- Focus on your purposes
- Focus your actions on your purposes.

Where business-building is concerned, how you structure your group is very important and can make the difference between a business with no firm foundation and one which is solid. Don't be too concerned about this at this stage. It will be fully covered later in the S.T.A.R. Leadership Programme, when the time is right. For now, keep yourself focused on sponsoring, retailing and teaching others the same, and...

Focus on your purpose

People get so bogged down in their actions that they forget what they are doing it all for. This is why, by using your Goals Sheet, I ask you to remind yourself of your goals *several times* each day. The more you Focus on what you want, from the business and from life, the more Drive you will have. Drive was the subject of Chapter 3. Drive is what makes you act. Drive is what makes things happen.

If you Focus so hard on your *actions* that you forget your *purposes*, you make the success or failure of each action important. This magnifies the importance of each obstacle you meet upon the way, so that failure in an action to overcome an obstacle may make you drop out. But, if you Focus on your purposes, then the failure of an action simply means that you will try another action and an obstacle means only something to be overcome to reach your goal.

Focus your actions on your purposes

Any action which does not lead directly to your goals is wasting valuable time as well as increasing your chances of failure. The difference between hard workers and hard, *smart* workers is that hard workers very often waste time and energy on the wrong actions. And, according to the Theory of Duplication, you are teaching your people to do the same... It is like setting off from London in the direction Brighton because you haven't properly planned your route to Edinburgh.

The way to make sure you are doing the right things at the right time is to *decide what your aims are, then plan how to achieve them by setting yourself targets.* That way, you are aiming your actions directly at your purposes. This has another advantage: if you write something down, you are more likely to do it and you are less likely to be sidetracked. This whole subject is covered in depth in my workbook *Target Success!* but, for now, I just want you to develop good habits of planning by setting yourself a few targets—targets which every serious distributor would want to set themselves:

Your Thirty-Minutes-A-Day Target. This is your target for daily study, which we covered on page 70.

Your BOM target. If your company holds these, go to one a week.

Your upline sizzle target. If your upline holds sizzle sessions, go to every one.

Your downline sizzle target. As soon as you have two distributors, start your own weekly sizzle session.

Your retailing target. How much must you sell each week to generate the immediate income you need? Base your target on that. If you do not need to make immediate income and are going to concentrate on sponsoring, you must still set a target even if it is only one order a week or a month. But bear in mind that the less retailing *you* do at this stage, the less well you will be able to teach retailing to your people.

Your contacting target. How many people will you contact each day to invite to a Two-to-One? Set a target you feel comfortable with. So many people blast off like a rocket, can't keep the pressure up and then drop out, victims of their own enthusiasm. This is a marathon, not a sprint; if your target proves too high, just reduce it because you must finish the race! If you do only three calls a day, that is still 90 a month!

I am closing your introduction to network marketing with *Focus on your purposes* and *Focus your actions on your purposes* because **they are the most important part of all the Six Winning Attitudes**. Why? Because they create your Drive. Drive is, and can only be, powered by what you want in life. The more you clarify and *make specific* what you want, and the more you *Focus* on what you want, the harder you will work and the quicker and the more certain you will make your success.

Leadership Quiz

Can you explain this chapter to other people? Yes—if you can answer these questions!

1 What is the Focusing attitude behind sponsoring?

2 What is the Focusing attitude behind retailing?

3 What is the Focusing attitude behind teaching?

4 Does Sponsor... Sponsor... Sponsor... mean sponsor only off your own Contact List?

5 Will you be more successful if you Focus on each action, or if you Focus on your purposes?

6 What are the two types of Focus which are the most important aspects of all the Six Winning Attitudes? Why?

7 What decides how strong your Drive will be?

8 Name two things which Drive will achieve.

Answers you should write down and refer to:

a One of your distributors refuses to Work With his people on their Contact Lists. What four reasons would you give him to change his mind?

b Although you cannot set retailing targets for your people, what four things, in retailing terms, can you expect of them?

Conclusion

The Way Ahead

Now that you are properly launched on the S.T.A.R. Leadership Programme, I would like to give you some advice about your next steps. The complete programme is:

1. *Get Off To A Winning Start In Network Marketing* (this book)

2. *Breakthrough Sponsoring & Retailing*

3. *How To Lead A Winning Group.*

Get Off To A Winning Start is exactly right to get you and your people off the ground, because it gives all the initial information you need in a very simple way. If you have just finished your first reading, you should read it again now, noting down action points as you go.

But also start reading and applying a good book on self-development. This can be my own book, *Network Marketeers—Supercharge Yourself!* the first personal development book written specifically to meet the needs of network marketeers. Or your uplines may recommend a more general book for you. Remember:

You can succeed only to the level of your personal development

---

The way to achieve more and to make your success more certain is through personal development. No matter how much you learn about sponsoring, retailing and teaching, about network marketing, about your product or your company, these are only the *tools* of your success. The *driving force* for your success is in your mind and *only* in your mind.

Perhaps you are one of those lucky few who have developed all the Winning Attitudes naturally. But, even if you do not need to study personal development techniques for yourself, you will find that *most of your people will* and, if you want to succeed, you should prepare yourself to help them.

If you have just finished your second reading of *How To Make A Winning Start*, now is the time to *Get-Active!* Work through the Action List on pages 4 and 5.

Treat yourself to a copy of my workbook, *Target Success!*. This will help you to complete your Contact List in the right way. It will also give you valuable advice on how you and your first distributors can harness the power of planning to drive you to success.

If you fail to plan, you are planning to fail

If you are new to self-employment, you may also need practical advice on administration, keeping accounts, setting up your home office, business cards, tax, VAT and so on. I give you help on all this in *Target Success!*.

You are now ready to read and apply the lessons in the second book of your home-learning course, *Breakthrough Sponsoring & Retailing*. But take your time over that. This is a marathon, not a sprint, so go at your own pace. Remember:

The important thing is not how long it takes you to learn, but that you *do* learn

---

And *please* do not yet open *How To Lead A Winning Group!* You are not quite ready yet to tackle that serious ski slope, but you soon will be!

Through the S.T.A.R. Leadership Programme I can provide everything else for you, but the one question I cannot answer is: Will you *do* it?

I hope that, now you understand what is involved, you are confident in feeling, 'I can!'.

From 'I can!', I hope that you soon progress to, 'I will!' because nothing would give me more pleasure than to welcome you into the great army of distributors the world over who have built for themselves the lifestyles they have chosen, or who found the answers to small or serious problems in their lives, all through network marketing.

Never lose sight of the fact that success does not have to mean reaching the top. It means deciding for yourself what your ATAC Equation is (what does **A**bundant **T**ime, **A**bundant **C**ash mean for *you*?), then solving it. It means deciding for yourself what you will find in the City of Dreams and then getting there. The distributors I am most inspired by are those who have achieved that for themselves, no matter if all it required was a small part-time income.

And never lose sight of the fact that your business will grow only as big as YOU grow. The goals you reach will be only as big as the goals that YOU dare to reach for. The inspiration you pass on to your people will be only as great as the inspiration that YOU develop for yourself. The level of integrity, caring and mutual support that develops in your people will be only as great as the integrity, caring and support which YOU learn to show in all of your business dealings. This is the most exciting, and scary, thing about running your own business: your business will become an expression of what YOU become.

Keep giving value, keep making people feel the better for your passing by, and you will reach whatever success you want in life—and, more importantly, you will feel justifiably proud of the contribution you have made to those around you. Than that, there is no finer accolade!

May your God or good fortune go with you.

Glossary

Terms used by the S.T.A.R. Leadership Programme

Any term in *italics* is defined elsewhere in this Glossary.

Applying The Six Winning Attitudes. One of the *Four Must-Do Activities* which drives the other three: Sponsoring, Retailing and Teaching. The six attitudes are: Be Patient; Have Drive; Be Hungry To Learn; Have Focus; Have Pride; People Buy People.

ATAC Equation. **A**bundant **T**ime, **A**bundant **C**ash. Each person's ideal lifestyle. The ATAC Equation is so-called because you can only solve it by ATTACKING the things in life which get in the way of it.

Co-learner. Another new distributor like yourself, working together with you to get your respective businesses going. You do not have to be in the same group.

Compatible Distributor. One to whom another distributor can relate because they have something in common such as the same background, occupation, ethnic group, age or sex, or have had to overcome the same problem.

Contact Box. A filing system used to follow up on a regular basis everyone you have contacted but who has not yet signed up as a distributor.

Figure-of-Eight Attitude. You are the focal point of the figure '8'. Above are your uplines, below are your downlines. You are the point of communication both ways (see diagram on page 69).

Four Must-Do Activities For Success. The essential activities of Sponsoring, Retailing, Teaching and the Applying The Six Winning Attitudes which drive them (driven in turn by the Keystone Law) (see diagram on page 9).

The S.T.A.R. Leadership Programme stands for **S**ponsoring, **T**eaching, **A**ttitudes, **R**etailing.

Goals Sheet. An inspiring summary of the most important, burning ambitions you aim to achieve through your business. To be referred to as often as possible, to feel that you have achieved your goals already and to keep yourself focused on your purposes.

Going Off-Track. Missing any one of the elements of *Staying On-Track*.

GUIDE Sequence. The Steps of the sponsoring process through which every contact has to go: **G**et-Active Step; **U**nfolding Step; **I**nvestigating Step; **D**ecision Step; **E**nsuing Step.

Keystone Law. Your path to success is ONLY through your people. The inspiration for the *Six Winning Attitudes*.

'Pigs Around The Corner'. Problems faced by *all* new distributors, who should therefore be warned about them.

Productive Distributor. A distributor who has signed up at least two people.

Staying On-Track. Putting in the time promised; willing to *Work With* and learn from their uplines; and willing to apply what they have learnt with the right attitudes, particularly Drive and Focus.

Thirty-Minutes-A-Day Habit. Thirty minutes a day of studying tapes, books and videos. Fifteen minutes should be spent on recapping, fifteen minutes on new study.

Training LLAWR. The sources of knowledge: **L**isten to successful distributors; **L**isten to tapes; **A**ttend meetings; **W**atch videos; **R**ead books.

Working With. Giving hands-on help in the field to everyone who is *Staying On-Track*.

Looking for the very best in British sponsoring and training aids?

Contact the Insight Network Marketing Library TODAY and we will tell you about:

- Our exciting range of NEW sponsoring and training materials featuring David Barber, Peter Clothier and Derek Ross

- David Barber's affordable *Momentum Generating Day* and other trainings by top British speakers

- Our mail order book and tape service for people experiencing difficulty in purchasing what they need through their network

- Volume supplies at generous discounts.

For friendly and helpful advice, just ring our orderline on

01989-564496

and we will send you:

- A FREE Catalogue
- A valuable bonus gift.

Or write to:

Insight Publishing Ltd
Sterling House
Church Street
Ross-on-Wye
Herefordshire
HR9 5HN

Group Leader?
Book Distributor?

We can supply this book at quantity discounts.

For further details, ring the Insight orderline on:

01989-564496